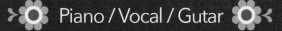

2nd Edition

POLKA TIME!

T0048224

ISBN 978-0-7935-0487-9

HAL•LEONARD®
CORPORATION
7777 W. BLUEMOUND RD. P.O. BOX 13819 MILWAUKEE, WI 53213

Visit Hal Leonard Online at
www.halleonard.com

CONTENTS

4   Barbara Polka

6   Beer Barrel Polka
    (Roll Out the Barrel)

11 The Chicken Dance

14 Clarinet Polka

16 Emilia Polka

19 The Happy Wanderer
    (Val-de-ri Val-de-ra)

22 Helena Polka

24 Hoop-Dee-Doo

29 Hop-Scotch Polka

32 In Heaven There
    Is No Beer

34 Jenny Lind Polka

36 Jolly Peter

40 Julida Polka

44 Just Another Polka

54 Just Because

56 Liechtensteiner Polka

49 The Merry Christmas Polka

60 (Put Another Nickel In) Music! Music! Music!

66 My Melody of Love

68 No Beer Today

63 Paloma Blanca

70 Pennsylvania Polka

75 Pizzicato Polka

78 Red Wing Polka

81 Schnitzelbank

84 There Is a Tavern in the Town

86 Tic-Tock Polka

98 Tinker Polka

88 Too Fat Polka (She's Too Fat for Me)

94 Vict'ry Polka

BARBARA POLKA

Traditional

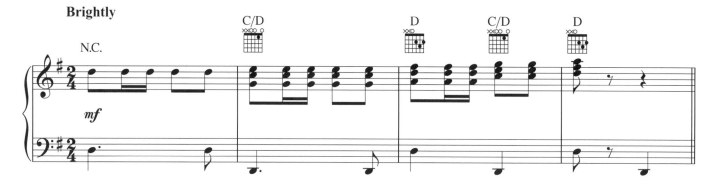

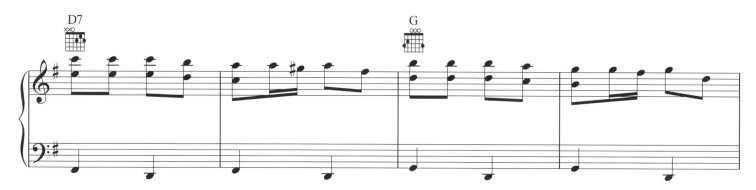

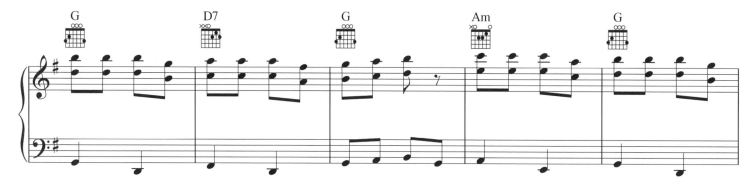

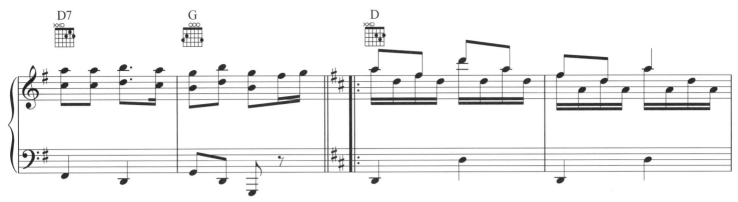

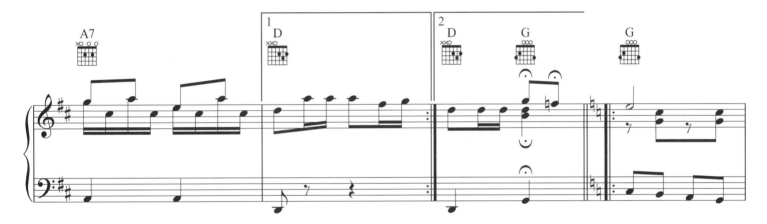

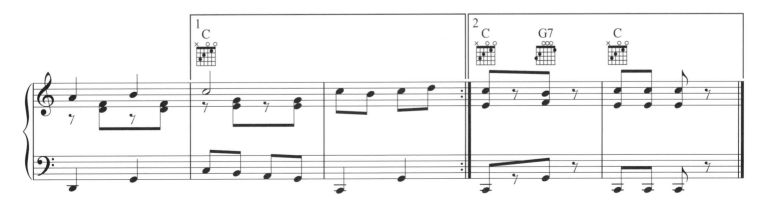

BEER BARREL POLKA
(Roll Out the Barrel)
Based on the European success "Skoda Lasky"*

By LEW BROWN, WLADIMIR A. TIMM,
JAROMIR VEJVODA and VASEK ZEMAN

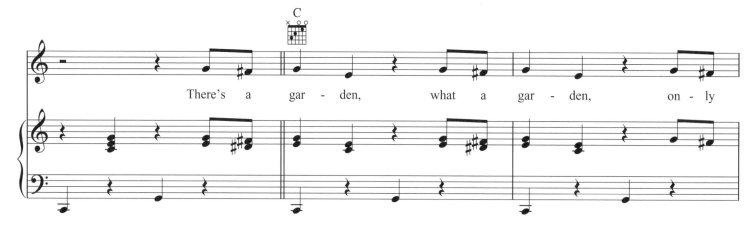

There's a gar-den, what a gar-den, on-ly

hap-py fac-es bloom there, and there's nev-er an-y

room there for a wor-ry, or a gloom there. Oh, there's

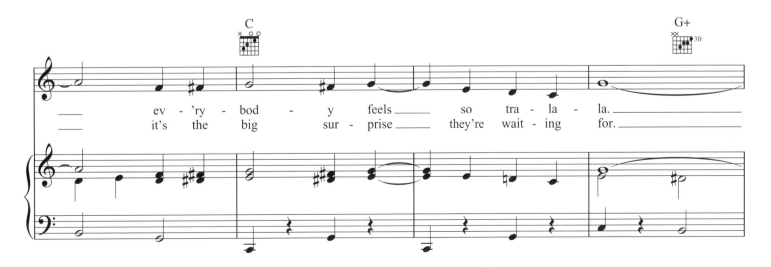

8

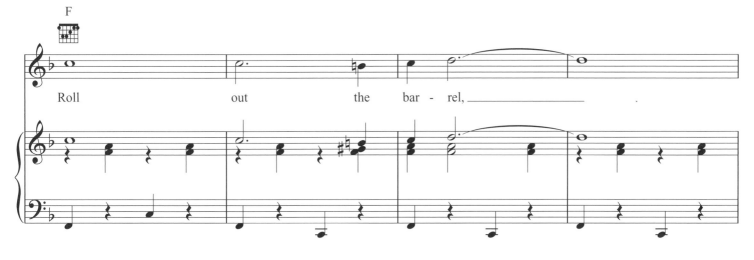

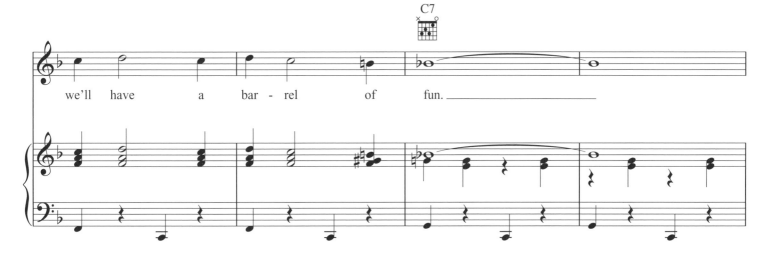

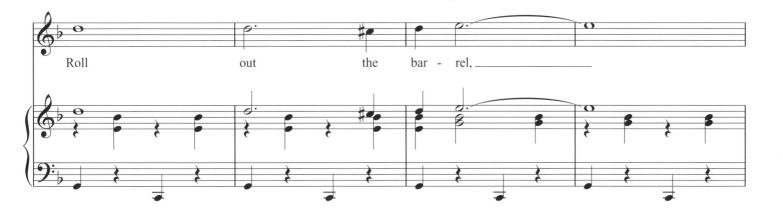

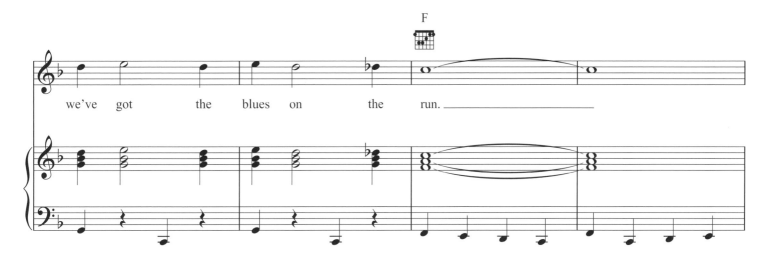

Zing! Boom! Ta - rar - rel! _____

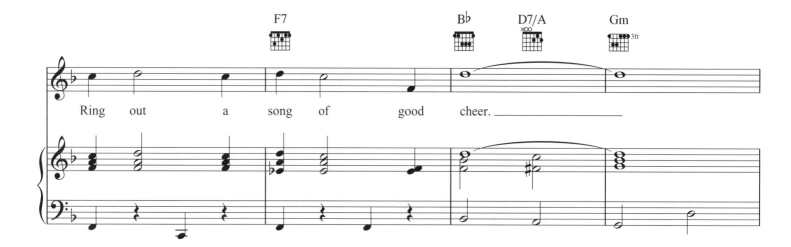

Ring out a song of good cheer. _____

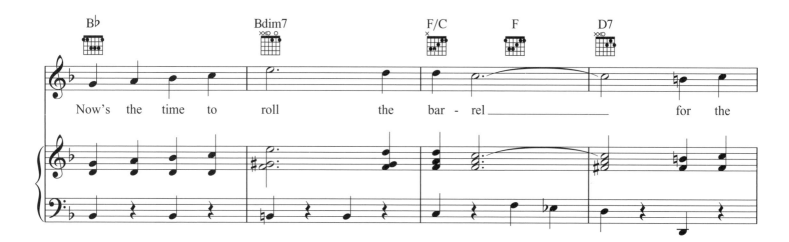

Now's the time to roll the bar - rel _____ for the

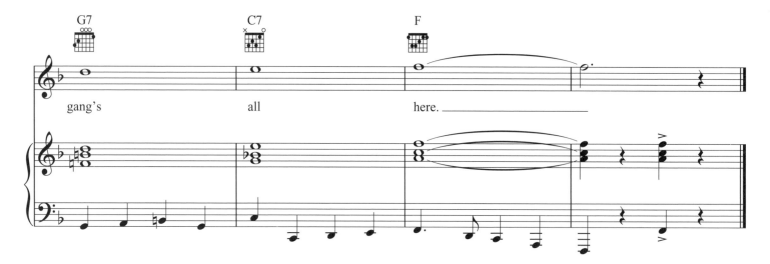

gang's all here. _____

THE CHICKEN DANCE

By TERRY RENDALL
and WERNER THOMAS
English Lyrics by PAUL PARNES

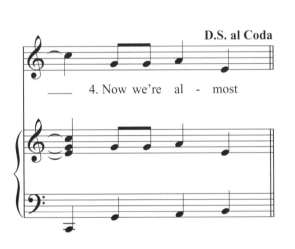

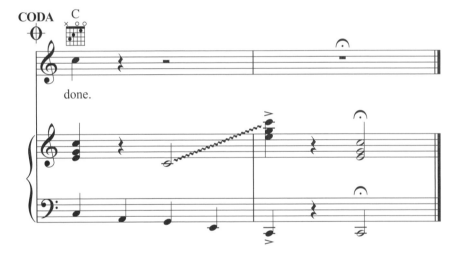

Additional Lyrics

2. Hey, you're in the swing.
   You're cluckin' like a bird. (Pluck, pluck, pluck, pluck.)
   You're flappin' your wings.
   Don't you feel absurd. (No, no, no, no.)
   It's a chicken dance,
   Like a rooster and a hen. (Ya, ya, ya, ya.)
   Flappy chicken dance;
   Let's do it again. *(To Chorus 2:)*

Chorus 2:
   Relax and let the music move you.
   Let all your inhibitions go.
   Just watch your partner whirl around you.
   We're havin' fun now; I told you so.

3. Now you're flappin' like a bird
   And you're wigglin' too. (I like that move.)
   You're without a care.
   It's a dance for you. (Just made for you.)
   Keep doin' what you do.
   Don't you cop out now. (Don't cop out now.)
   Gets better as you dance;
   Catch your breath somehow.
   Chorus

4. Now we're almost through,
   Really flyin' high. (Bye, bye, bye, bye.)
   All you chickens and birds,
   Time to say goodbye. (To say goodbye.)
   Goin' back to the nest,
   But the flyin' was fun. (Oh, it was fun.)
   Chicken dance was the best,
   But the dance is done.

CLARINET POLKA

Traditional

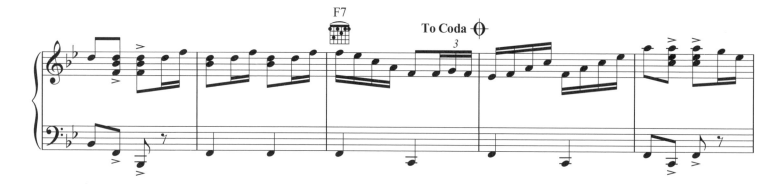

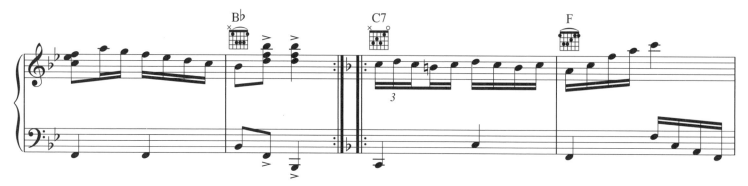

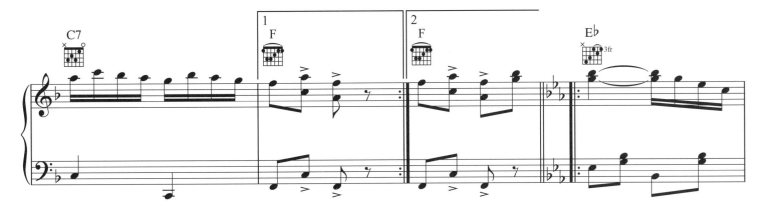

EMILIA POLKA

Words and Music by OLIVER DITSON
and EDUARDO BARREJON

There's a girl, there's a

girl that I keep think-ing of: E - mi - lia, my love, E-

mi - lia, my love. And the stars in the sky and the moon shines a -

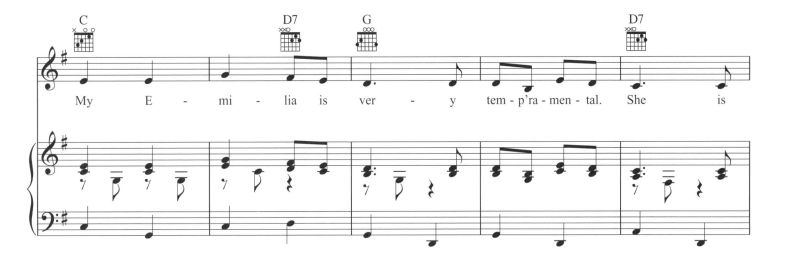

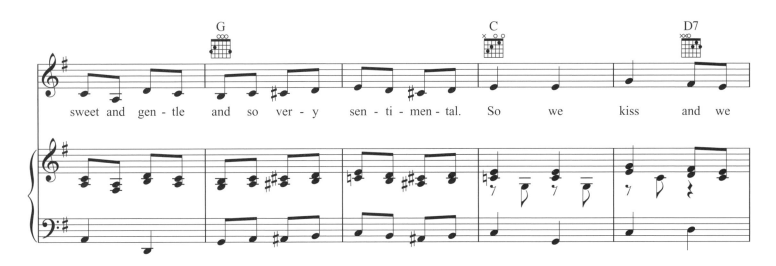

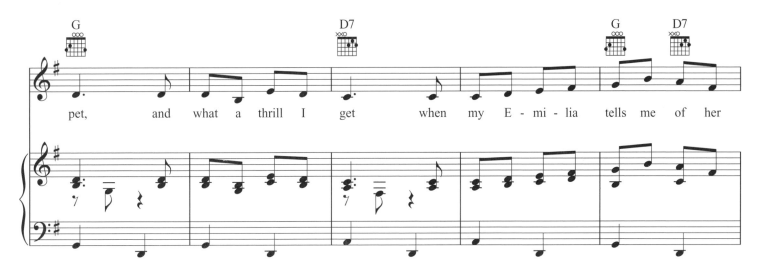

love.
Laugh with me, E - mi - lia, ha ha ha.
Laugh with me, E - mi - lia, ha ha ha.

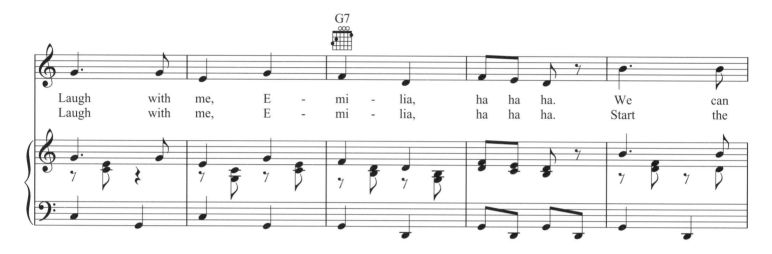

Laugh with me, E - mi - lia, ha ha ha. We can
Laugh with me, E - mi - lia, ha ha ha. Start the

laugh at rain - y weath - er, ha ha ha, long as we're to -
day with joy and laugh - ter, ha ha ha. Laugh, it's

geth - er, ha ha ha.
fun to be in love.

THE HAPPY WANDERER
(Val-de-ri Val-de-ra)

Words and Music by
FRIEDRICH MOELLER
English Lyrics by ANTONIA RIDGE

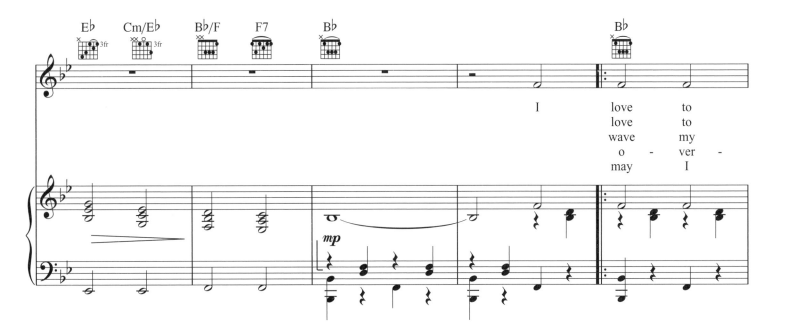

I love to
love to
wave my
o - ver -
may I

go a - wan - der - ing a - long the moun - tain
wan - der by the stream that danc - es in the
hat to all I meet, and they wave back to
head, the sky - larks wing; they nev - er rest at
go a - wan - der - ing un - til the day I

track. _____ And as I go, I love to
sun. _____ So joy - ous - ly it calls to
me. _____ And black - birds call so loud and
home. _____ But just like me, they love to
die! _____ Oh, may I al - ways laugh and

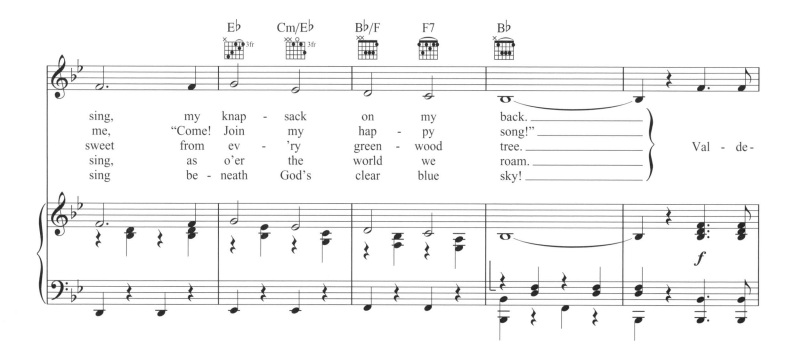

sing, my knap - sack on my back. _____
me, "Come! Join my hap - py song!" _____
sweet from ev - 'ry green - wood tree. _____
sing, as o'er the world we roam. _____
sing be - neath God's clear blue sky! _____ Val - de-

tra la la la la _____ tra la la la la _____ val - de-
ri, _____ val - de - ra, _____ val - de-

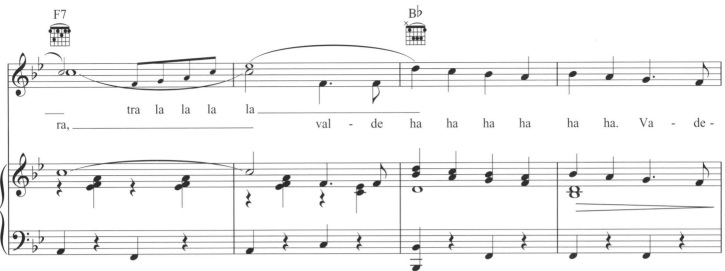

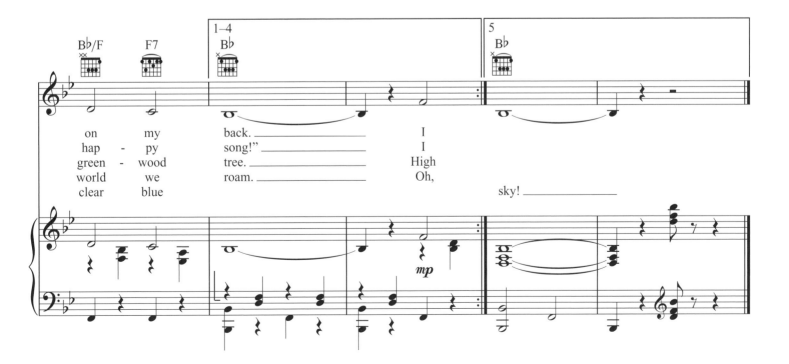

HELENA POLKA

Traditional

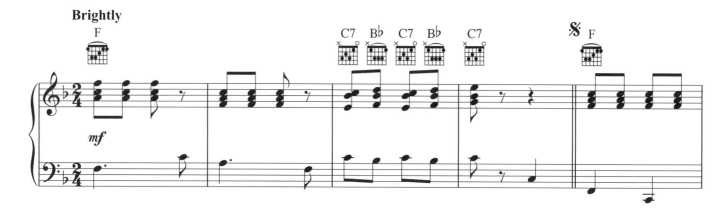

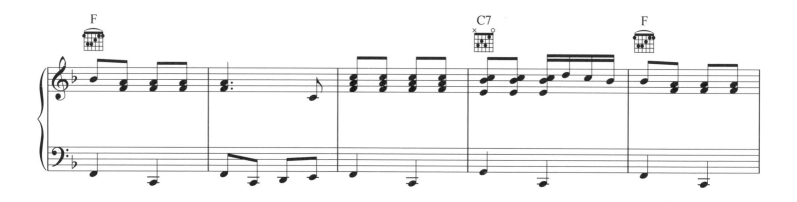

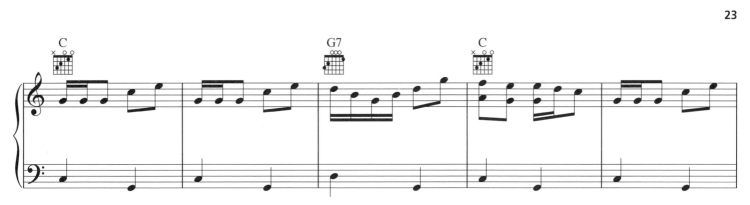
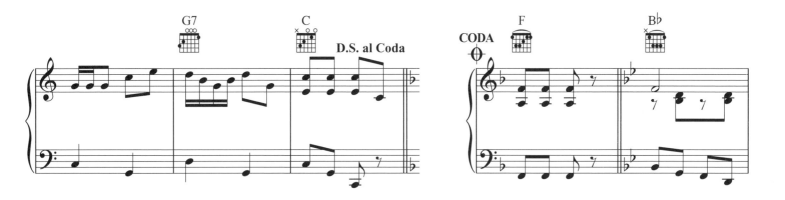

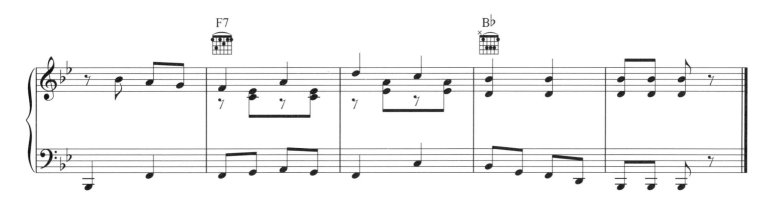

HOOP-DEE-DOO

Words by FRANK LOESSER
Music by MILTON DeLUGG

Hoop - dee - doo, hoop - dee - doo, I hear a pol - ka and my trou - bles are through. __ Hoop - dee - doo, hoop - dee - dee, this kind of mu - sic is like

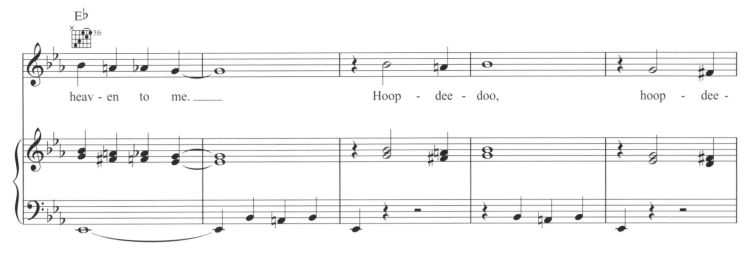

heav - en to me. _____ Hoop - dee - doo, hoop - dee -

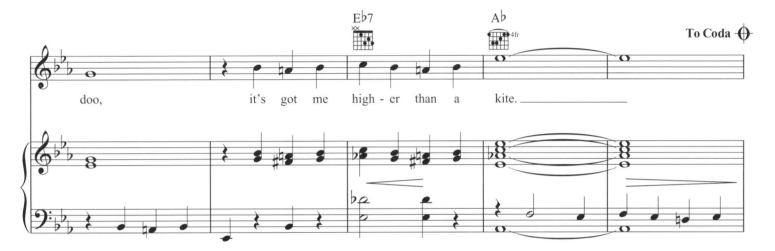

doo, it's got me high - er than a kite. _____

To Coda ⊕

Hand me down my soup and fish, I am gon - na get my wish

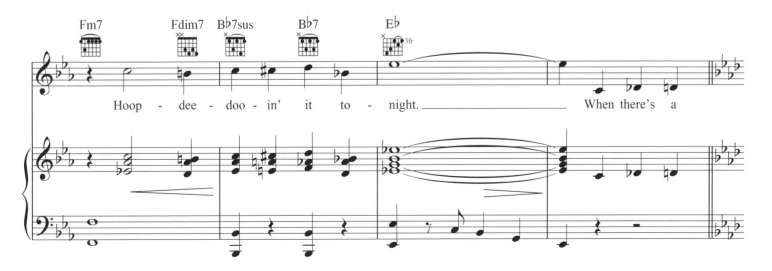

Hoop - dee - doo - in' it to - night. _____ When there's a

Trio

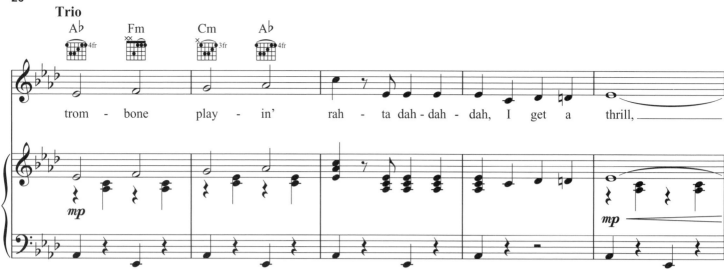

trom - bone play - in' rah - ta dah-dah-dah, I get a thrill, _____

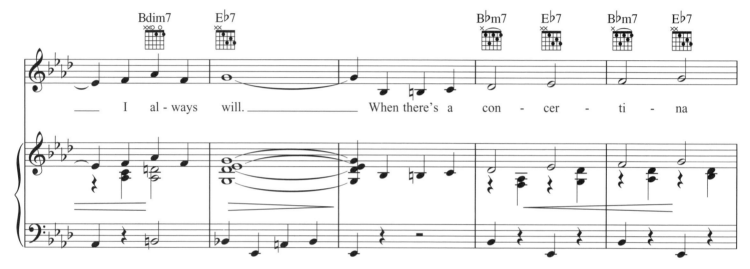

_____ I al - ways will. _____ When there's a con - cer - ti - na

stretch - in' out a mile, I al - ways smile, _____ 'cause that's my

style. _____ When there's a fid - dle in the mid - dle and he

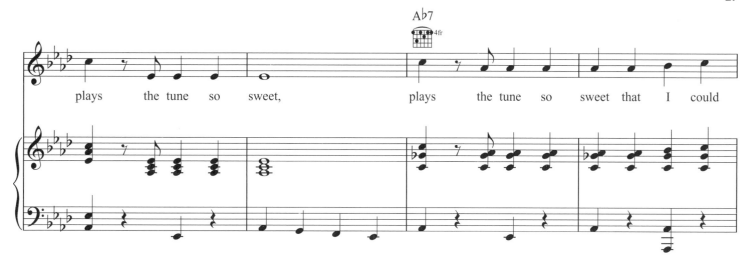

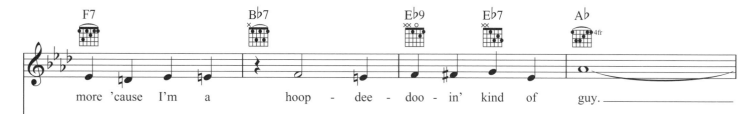

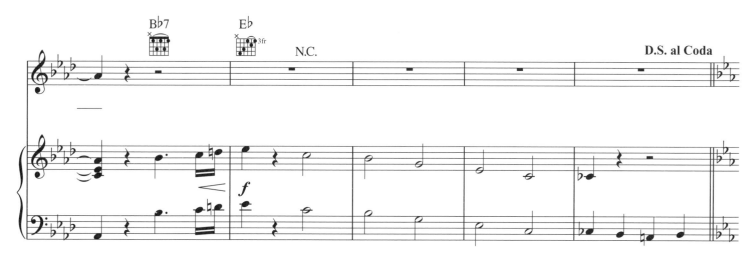

28

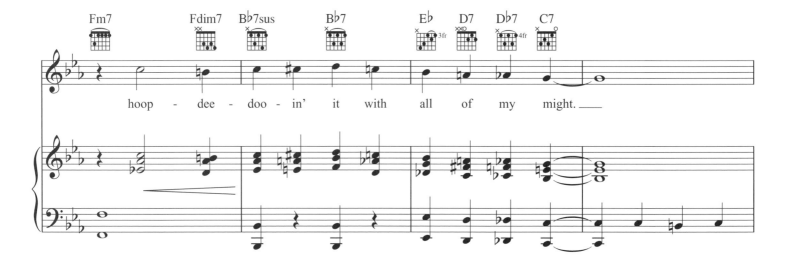

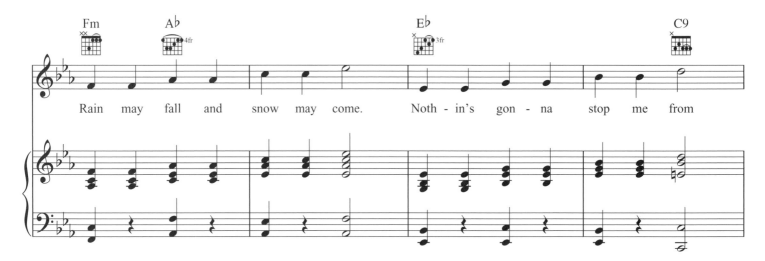

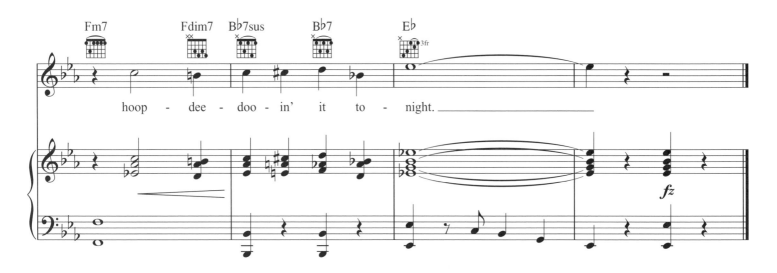

HOP-SCOTCH POLKA

Words and Music by CARL SIGMAN,
GENE RAYBURN and WILLIAM WHITLOCK

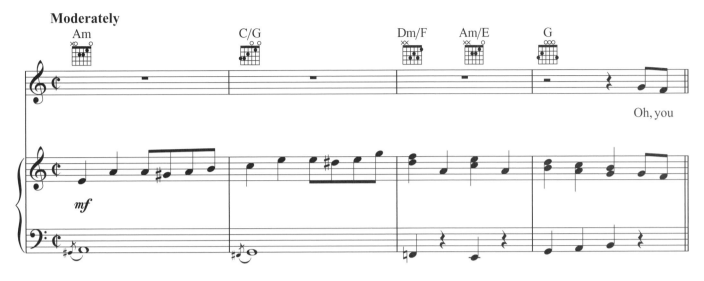

Oh, you

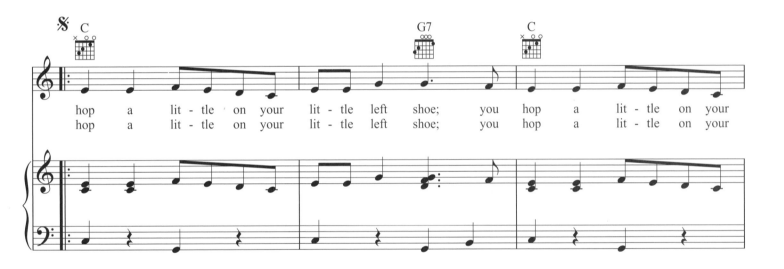

hop a lit-tle on your lit-tle left shoe; you hop a lit-tle on your
hop a lit-tle on your lit-tle left shoe; you hop a lit-tle on your

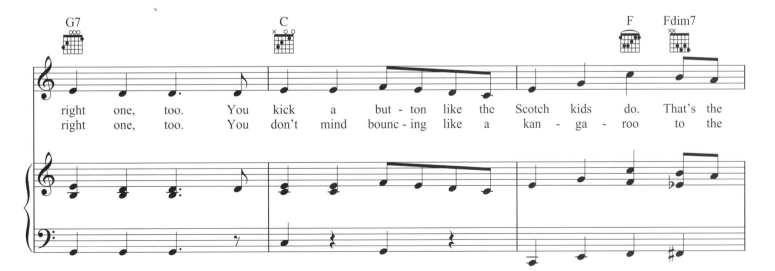

right one, too. You kick a but-ton like the Scotch kids do. That's the
right one, too. You don't mind bounc-ing like a kan-ga-roo to the

right one, too. You kick a but-ton like the Scotch kids do. That's the Hop - scotch

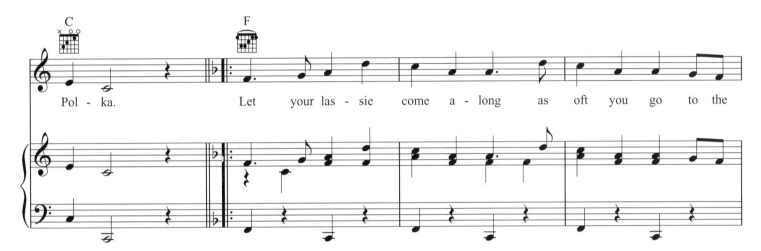

Pol - ka. Let your las - sie come a - long as oft you go to the

hop - scotch song. Sing - a - ligh and sing - a - lee, it's the hop - scotch mel - o -

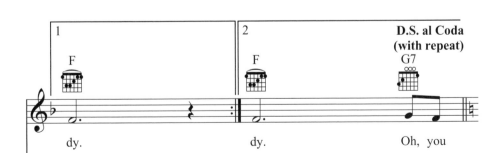

dy. dy. Oh, you

D.S. al Coda
(with repeat)

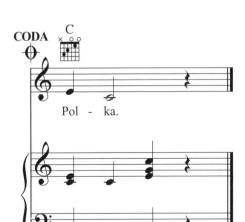

Pol - ka.

IN HEAVEN THERE IS NO BEER

Words and Music by RALPH MARIA SIEGEL
and ERNST NEUBACH

Bright Polka

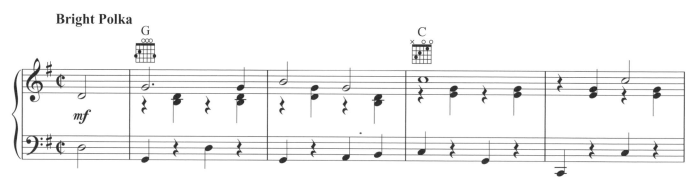

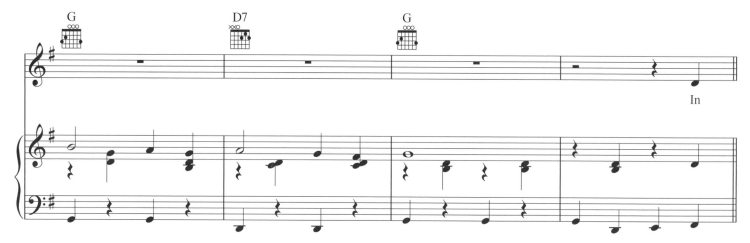

Heav - en, there is no beer; that's

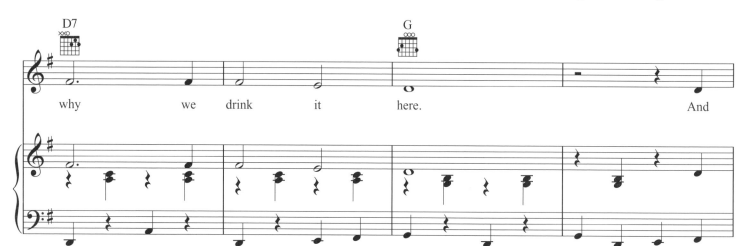

why we drink it here. And

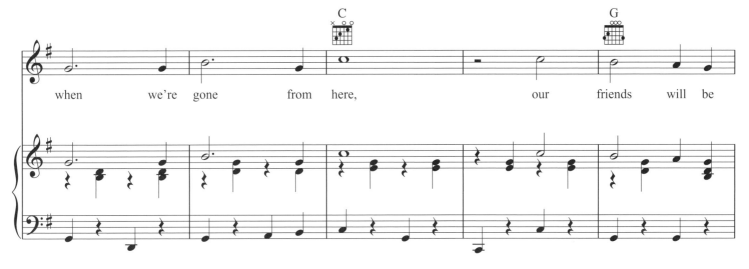

when we're gone from here, our friends will be

drink - ing all our beer. In

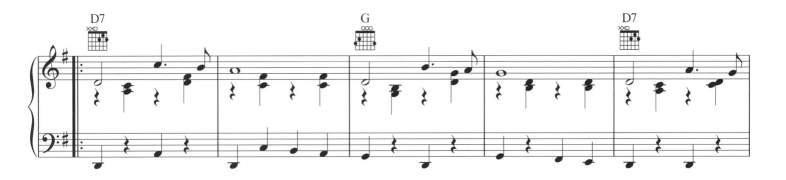

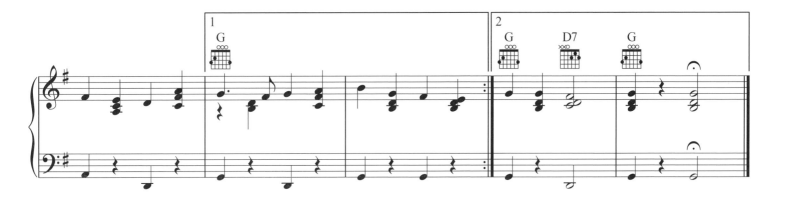

JENNY LIND POLKA

By ALLEN DODWORTH

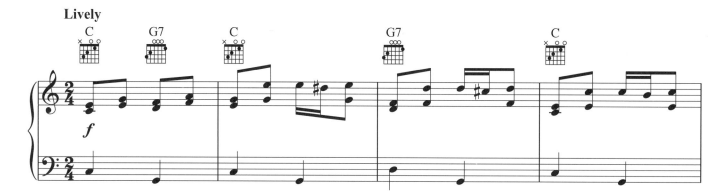

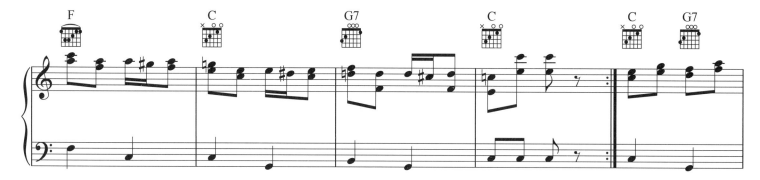

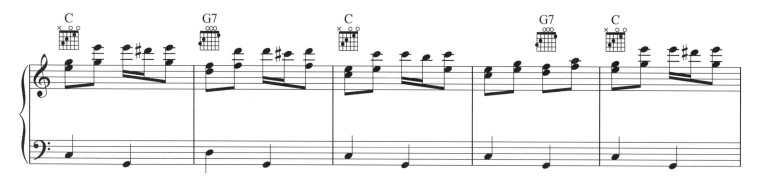

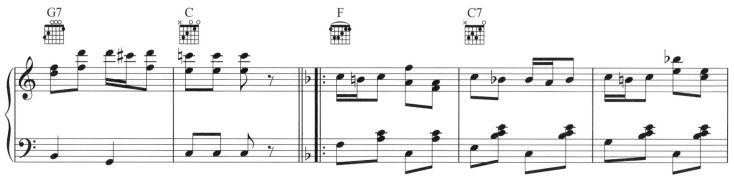

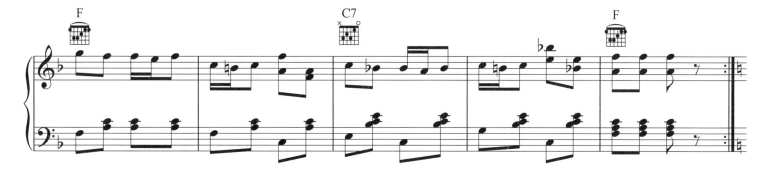

JOLLY PETER

By JOHN A. BASSETT
and M. WERNER-KERSTEN

With movement

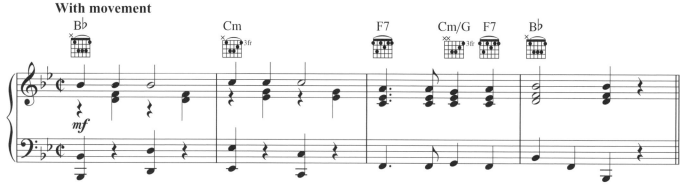

Jol - ly Pe - ter has a lit - tle stand in the zoo, right o - ver near the band,

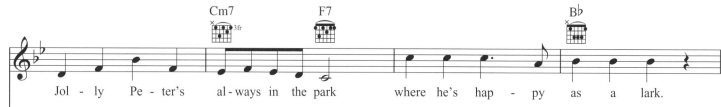

Jol - ly Pe - ter's al - ways in the park where he's hap - py as a lark.

Ev - 'ry day that's bright and fair, all the chil - dren gath - er there.

He's too fat to reach the shelf, so he says, "Go help your- self." But

keep it dark, is he an eas- y mark!

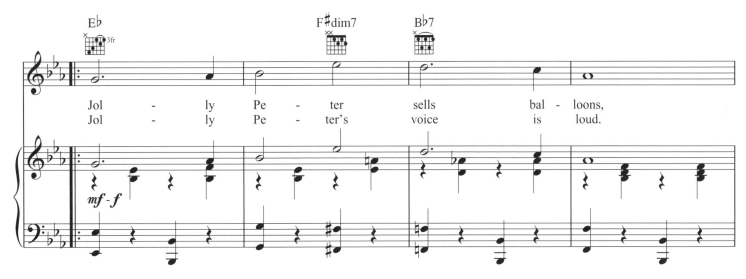

Jol - ly Pe - ter sells bal - loons,
Jol - ly Pe - ter's voice is loud.

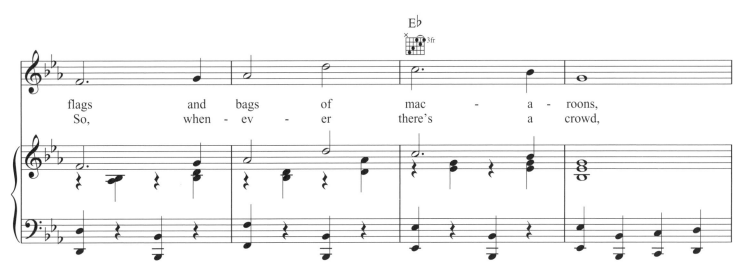

flags and bags of mac - a - roons,
So, when- ev - er there's a crowd,

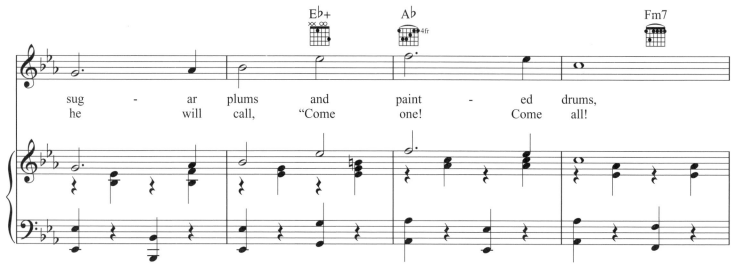

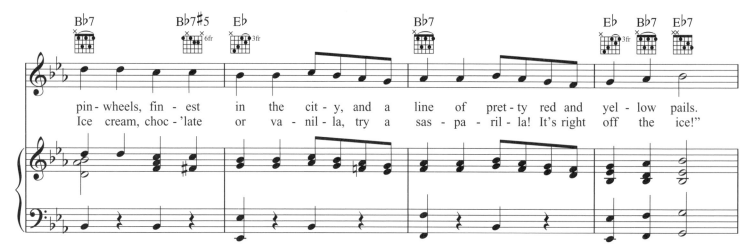

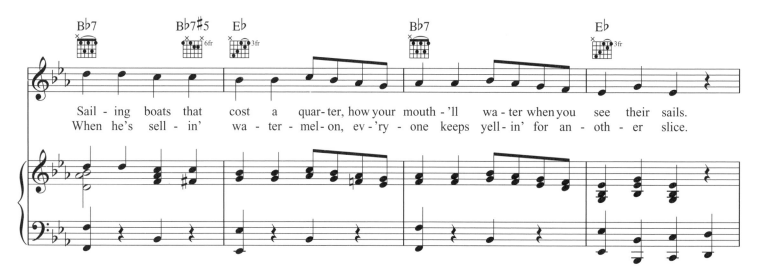

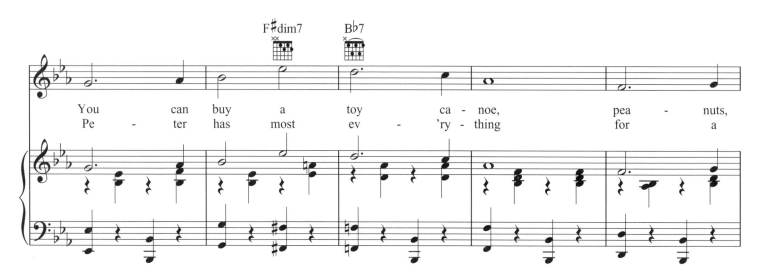

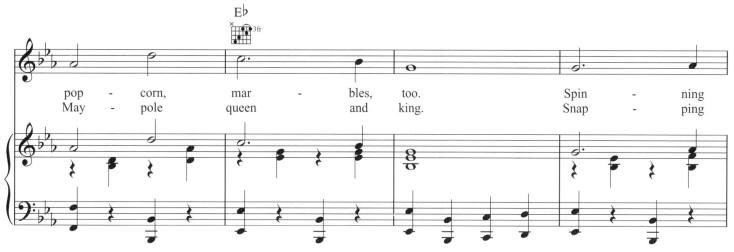

pop - corn, mar - bles, too. Spin - ning
May - pole queen and king. Snap - ping

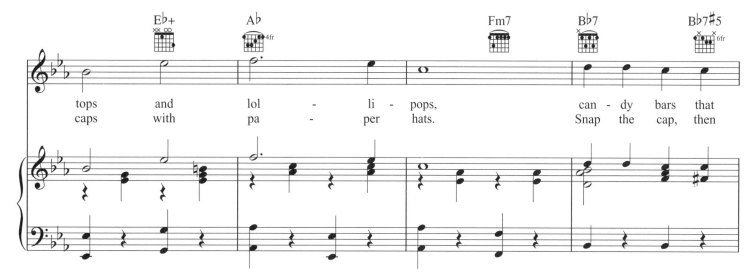

tops and lol - li - pops, can - dy bars that
caps with pa - per hats. Snap the cap, then

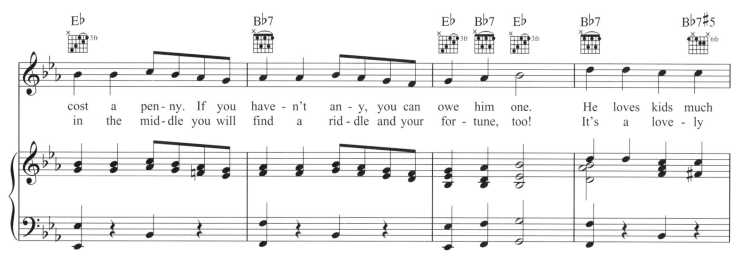

cost a pen - ny. If you have - n't an - y, you can owe him one. He loves kids much
in the mid - dle you will find a rid - dle and your for - tune, too! It's a love - ly

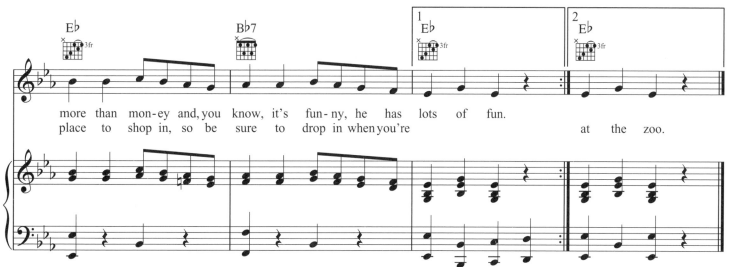

more than mon - ey and, you know, it's fun - ny, he has lots of fun.
place to shop in, so be sure to drop in when you're   at the zoo.

JULIDA POLKA

By A. GRILL

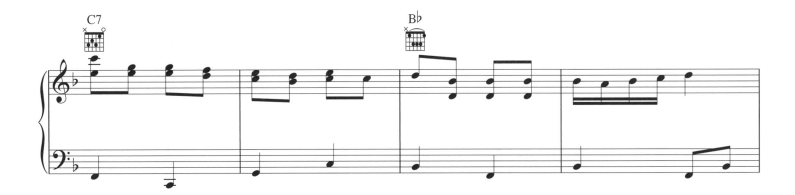

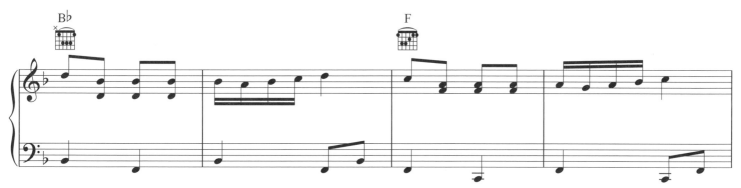

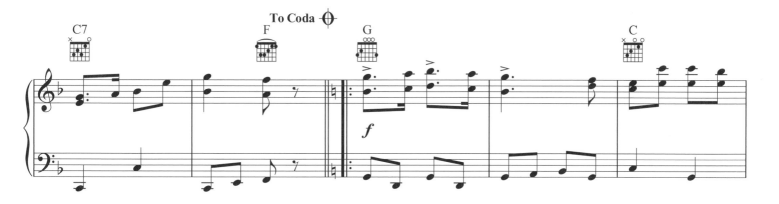

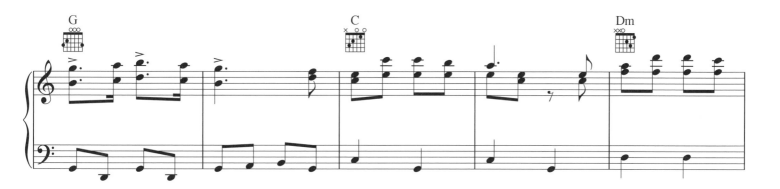

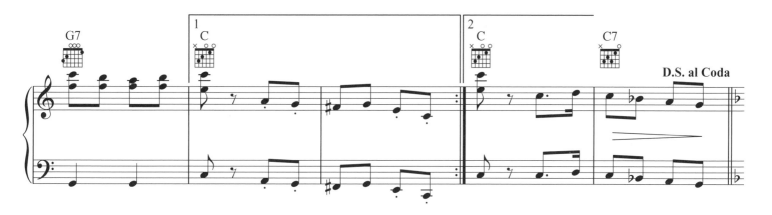

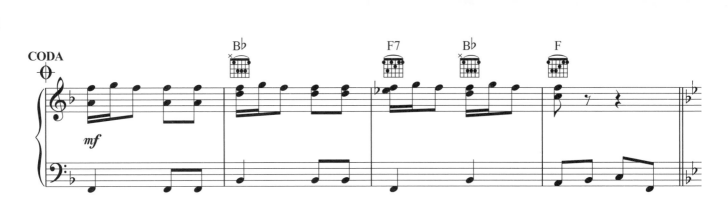

Trio

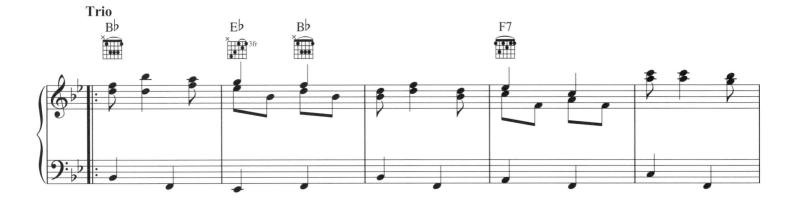

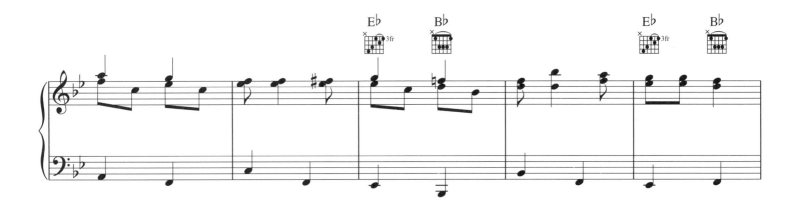

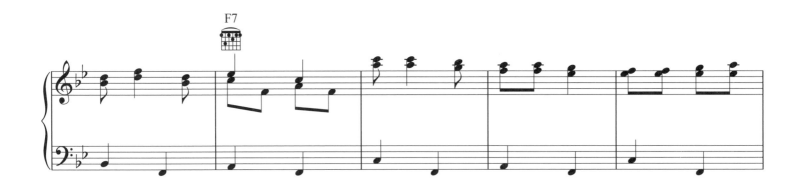

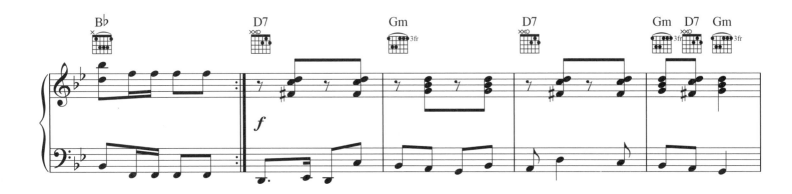

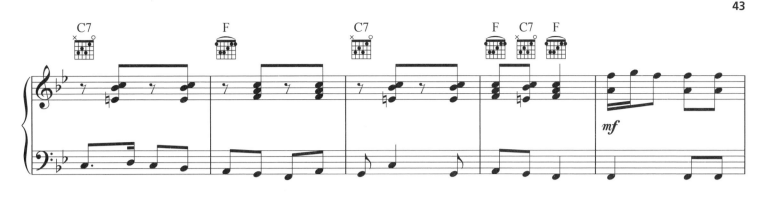

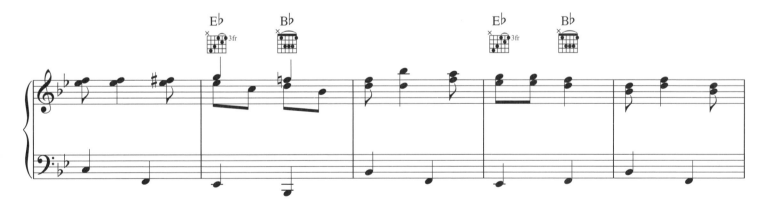

JUST ANOTHER POLKA

Words and Music by FRANK LOESSER
and MILTON DeLUGG

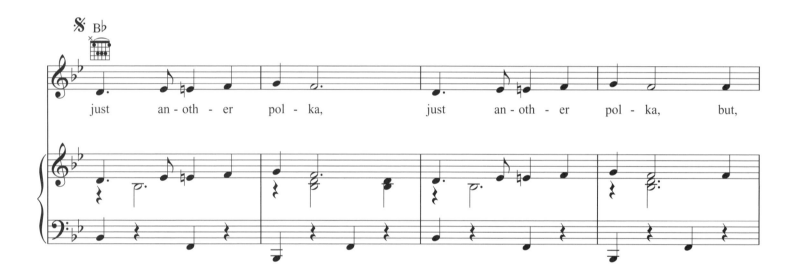

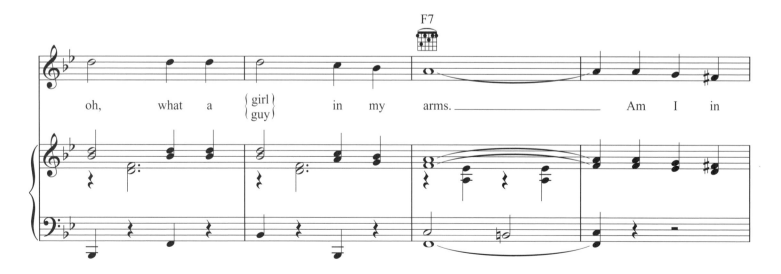

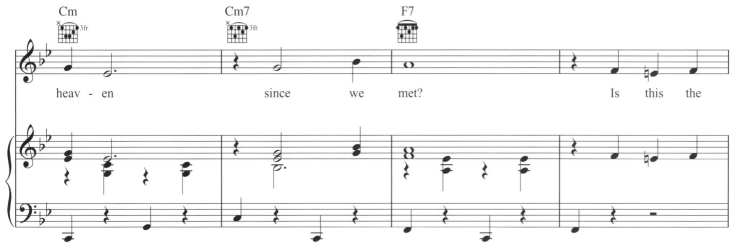

heav - en   since we met?   Is this the

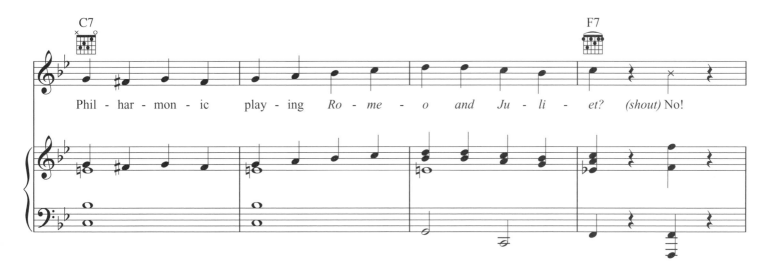

Phil - har - mon - ic play - ing *Ro - me - o and Ju - li - et?* (shout) No!

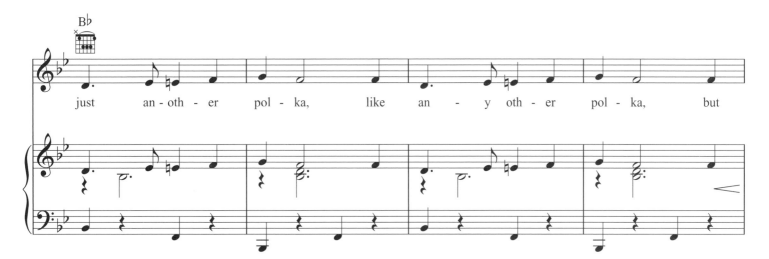

just an - oth - er pol - ka, like an - y oth - er pol - ka, but

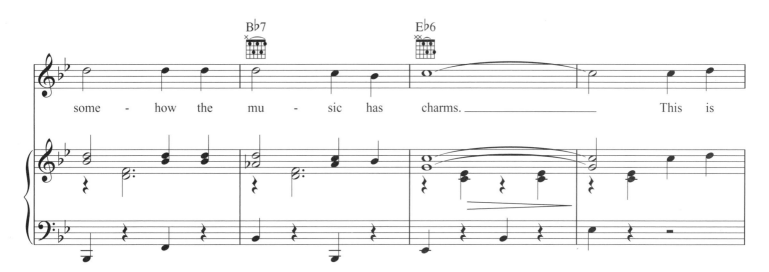

some - how the mu - sic has charms. _____ This is

46

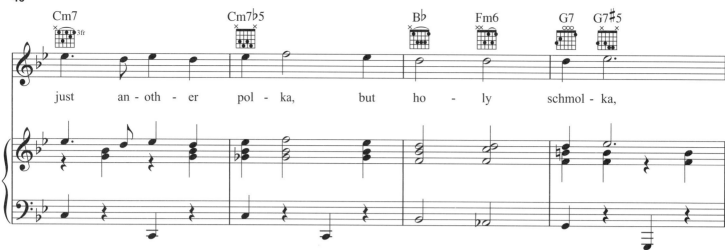

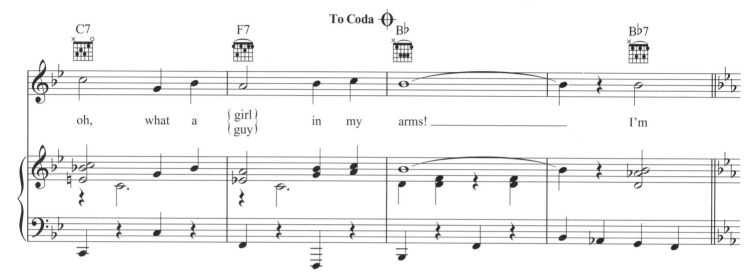

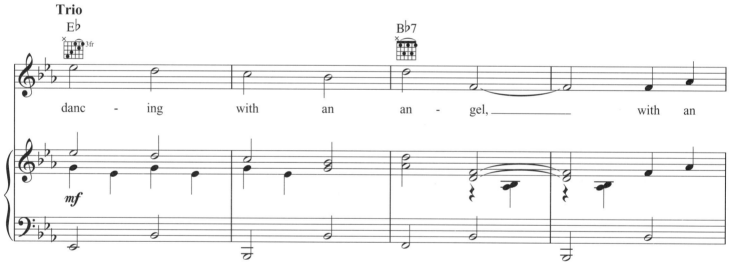

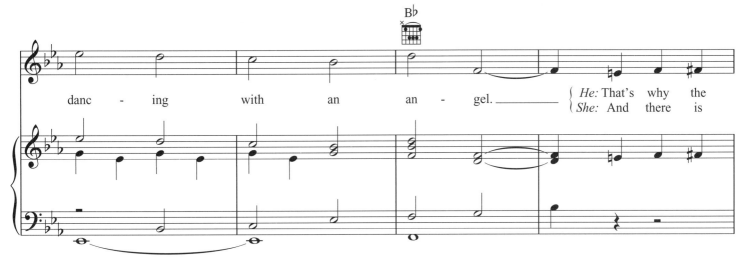

dance - ing with an an - gel. _____ *He:* That's why the
She: And there is

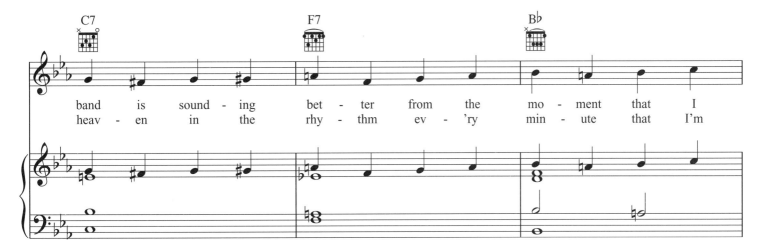

band is sound - ing bet - ter from the mo - ment that I
heav - en in the rhy - thm ev - 'ry min - ute that I'm

met her.} 'Cause I'm danc - ing with an an - gel, _____
with 'im.}

_____ with an an - gel, an an - gel, an an - gel. _____

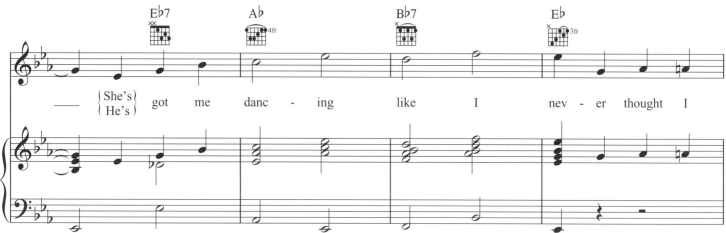

She's
He's got me danc - ing like I nev - er thought I

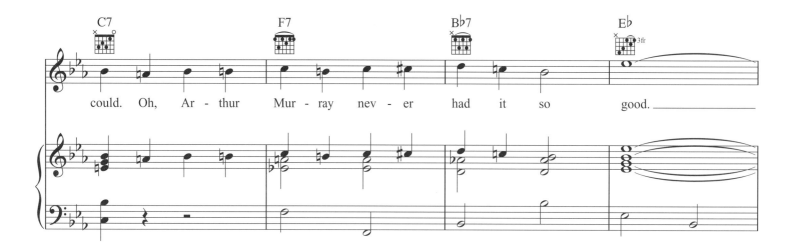

could. Oh, Ar - thur Mur - ray nev - er had it so good. _____

D.S. al Coda

_____ This is

CODA

(play it a - gain!) _____

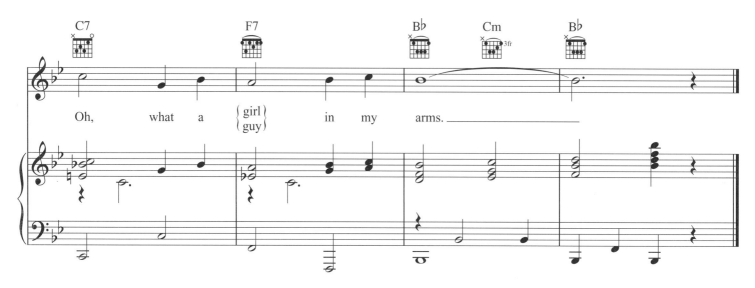

Oh, what a girl
guy in my arms. _____

THE MERRY CHRISTMAS POLKA

Words by PAUL FRANCIS WEBSTER
Music by SONNY BURKE

Moderate Polka tempo

They're

tun - ing up the fid - dles now, the fid - dles now, the fid - dles now. There's

wine to warm the mid - dles now and set your head a - whirl. A-

round and 'round the room we go, the room we go, the room we go, a-

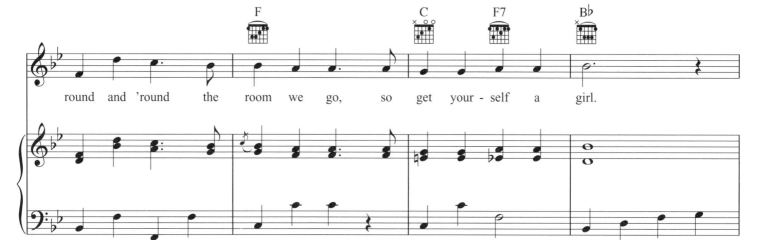

round and 'round the room we go, so get your-self a girl.

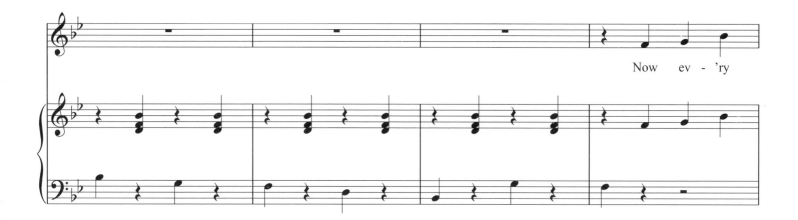

Now ev - 'ry

heart will start to tin - gle, when sleigh - bells

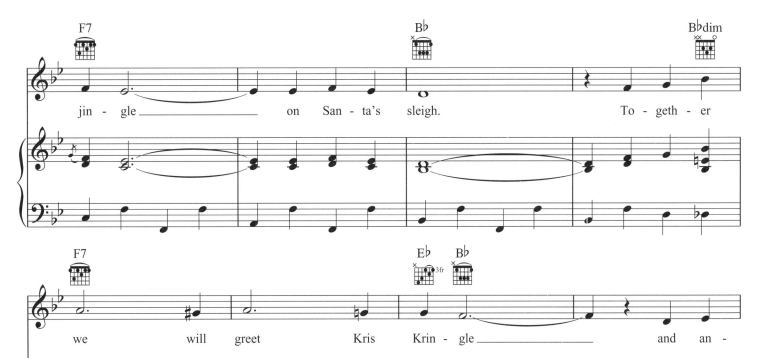

jin - gle _____ on San - ta's sleigh. To - geth - er

we will greet Kris Krin - gle _____ and an -

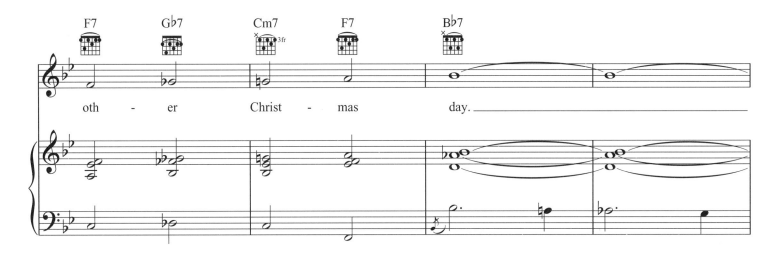

oth - er Christ - mas day. _____

Brightly

Come on and dance The Mer - ry Christ - mas
dance The Mer - ry Christ - mas

Pol - ka;   let ev - 'ry - one   be   hap - py   and
Pol - ka;   let ev - 'ry la - dy   step with   her

gay. _____ Oh! it's the time   to be   jol - ly   and
beau _____ a - round a tree   to the   ceil - ing   with

deck   the halls with hol - ly,   so   let's have   a   jol - ly hol - i -
lots   of time for steal - ing   those kiss - es   be - neath the mis - tle -

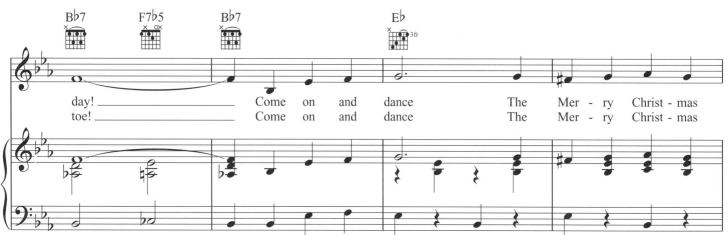

day! _____ Come on and dance The Mer - ry Christ - mas
toe! _____ Come on and dance The Mer - ry Christ - mas

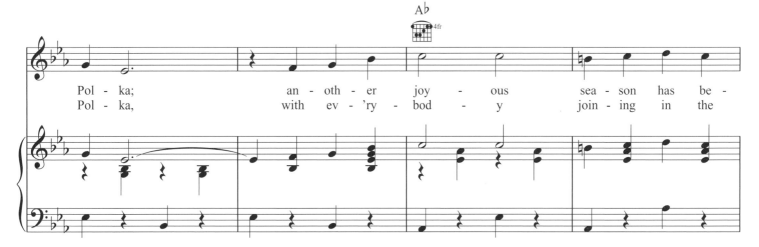

Pol - ka; an - oth - er joy - ous sea - son has be -
Pol - ka, with ev - 'ry - bod - y join - ing in the

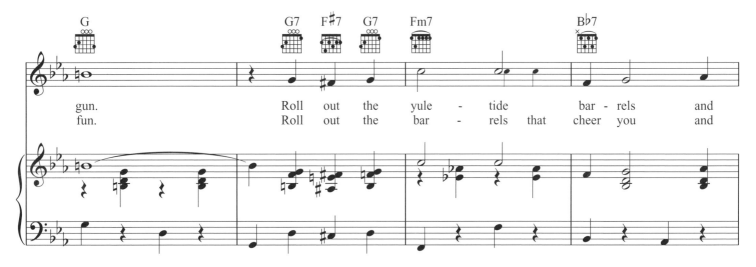

gun. Roll out the yule - tide bar - rels and
fun. Roll out the bar - rels that cheer you and

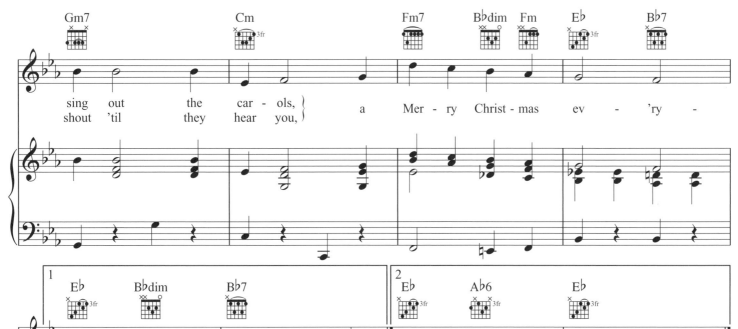

sing out the car - ols, } a Mer - ry Christ - mas ev - 'ry -
shout 'til they hear you, }

one! Come on and one! _____

JUST BECAUSE

Words and Music by BOB SHELTON,
JOE SHELTON and SID ROBIN

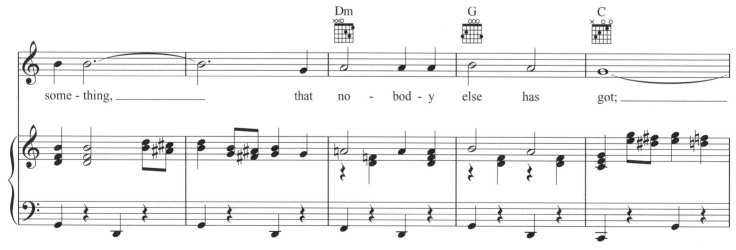

though you made me spend all my mon - ey,

you laughed and called me old San - ta Claus,

but I'm tell - ing you, hon - ey, I'm leav - ing

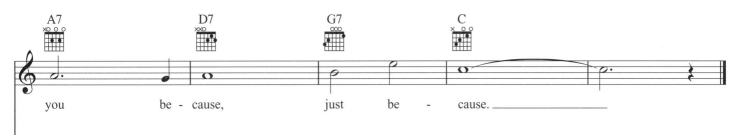

you be - cause, just be - cause.

LIECHTENSTEINER POLKA

Words and Music by EDMUND KOETSCHER
and RUDI LINDT

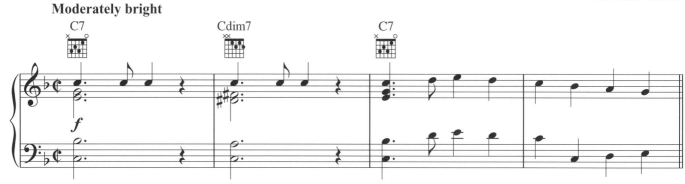

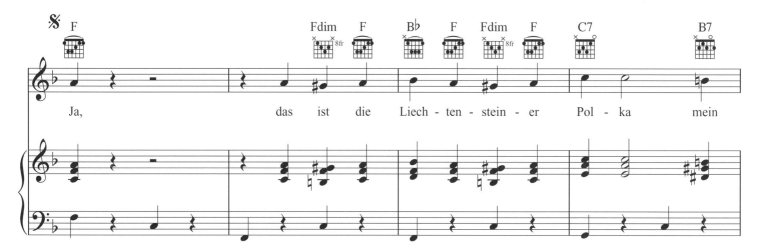

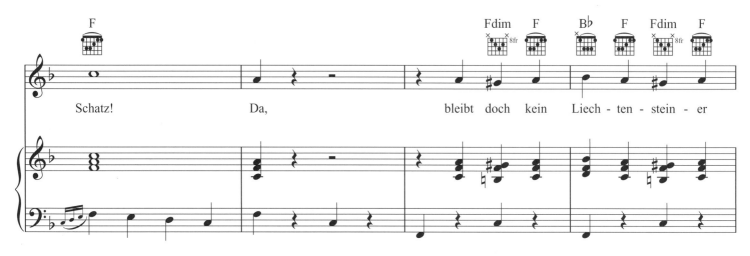

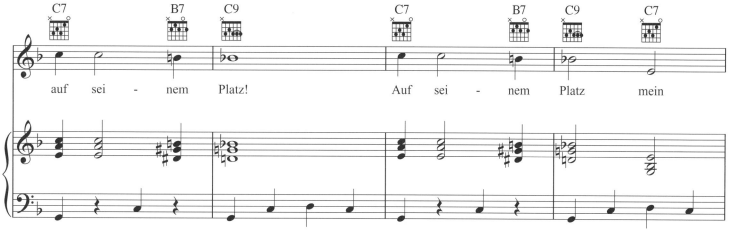

auf sei - nem Platz! Auf sei - nem Platz mein

Schatz! Man kann beim Schie - ben, Schie - ben, Schie - ben sich in

bei - de Au - gen seh'n. Man muß sich lie - ben, lie - ben, lie - ben, und die

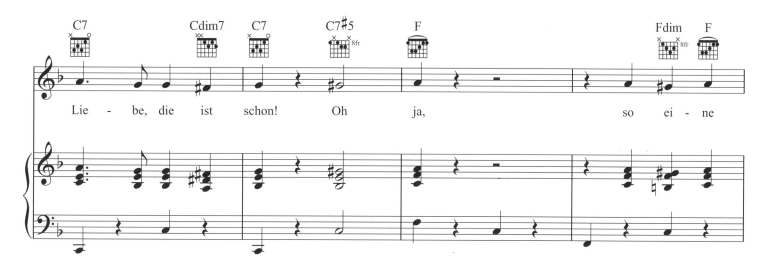

Lie - be, die ist schon! Oh ja, so ei - ne

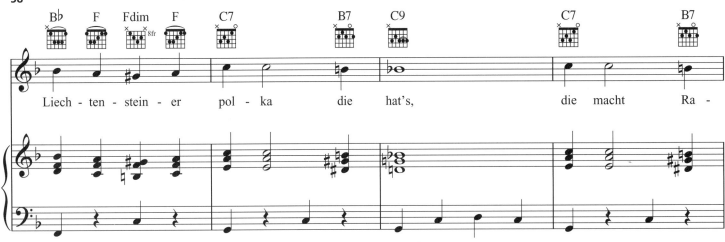

Liech - ten - stein - er pol - ka die hat's, die macht Ra -

batz, mein Schatz!

Der al - te Herr von Liech - ten - stein, Ja! Ja!

Ja! Der konn - te nicht al - lei - ne sein, Nein! Nein!

Nein! Er schick - te sei - ne Bo - ten aus, Ja! Ja!

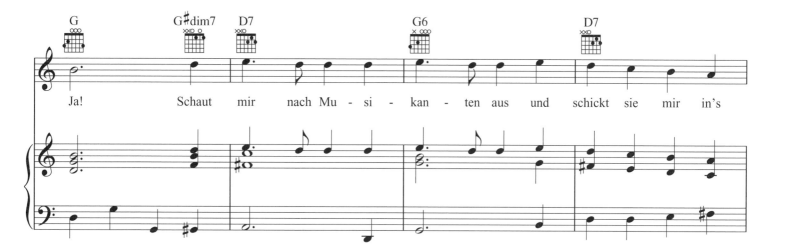

Ja! Schaut mir nach Mu - si - kan - ten aus und schickt sie mir in's

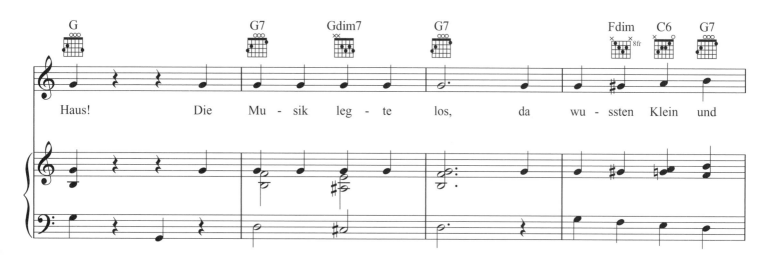

Haus! Die Mu - sik leg - te los, da wu - ssten Klein und

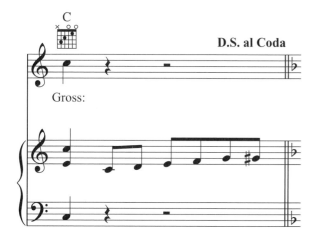

Gross:

D.S. al Coda

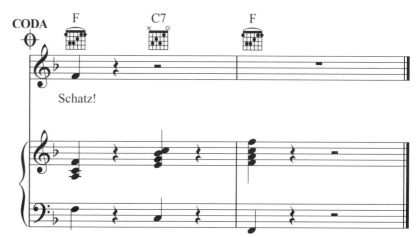

CODA

Schatz!

(Put Another Nickel In)
MUSIC! MUSIC! MUSIC!

Words and Music by STEPHAN WEISS
and BERNIE BAUM

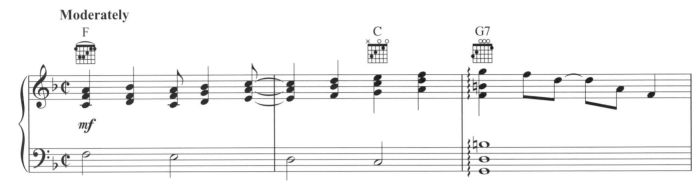

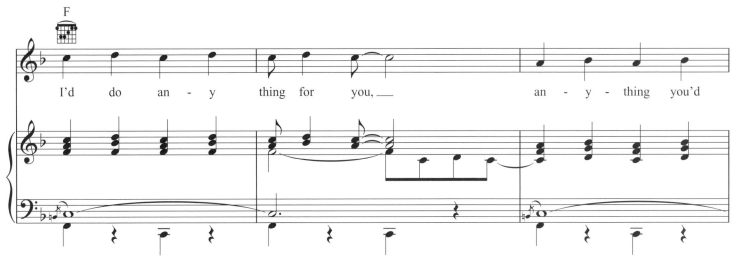

I'd do an-y thing for you, ___ an - y - thing you'd

want me to. ___ All I want is kiss - ing you ___ and

mu - sic! mu - sic! mu - sic! Clos - er, ___

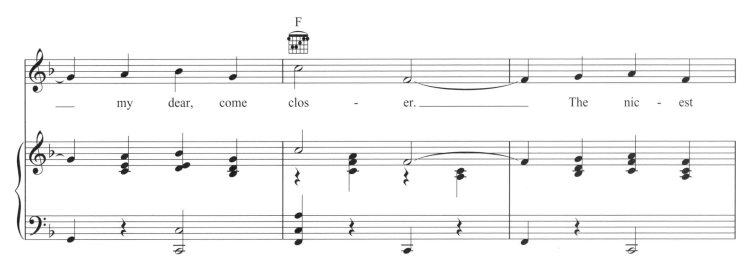

___ my dear, come clos - er. ___ The nic - est

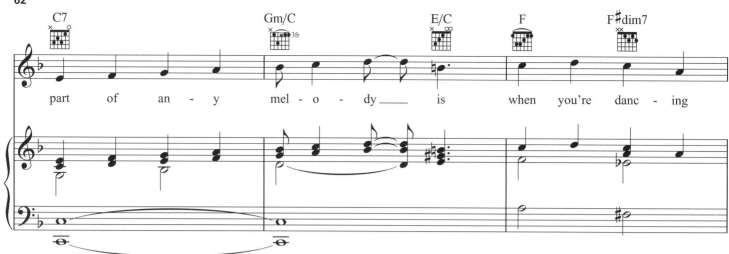

part of an - y mel - o - dy ___ is when you're danc - ing

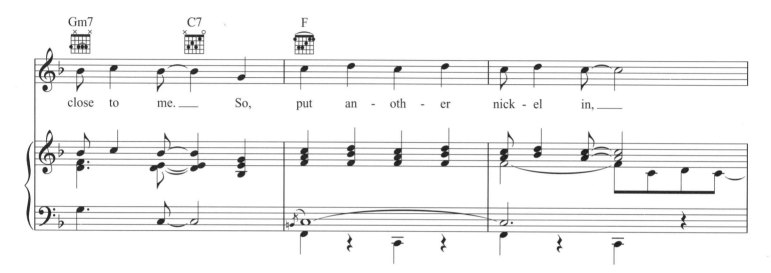

close to me. ___ So, put an - oth - er nick - el in, ___

in the nick - el - o - de - on. ___ All I want is

lov - ing you ___ and mu - sic! mu - sic! mu - sic! mu - sic!

PALOMA BLANCA

Words and Music by
HANS BOUWENS

When the

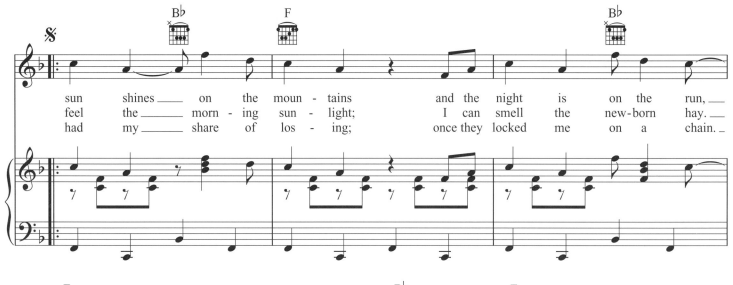

U - na pa - lo - ma blan - ca,

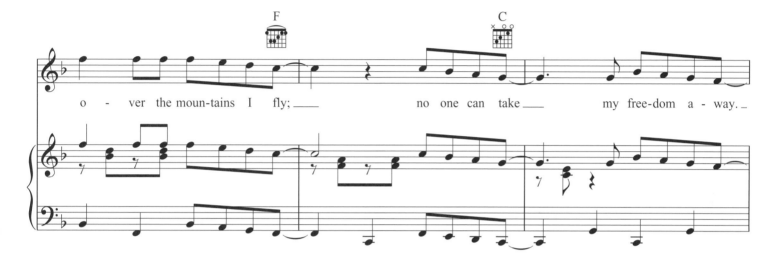

o - ver the moun-tains I fly; ___ no one can take ___ my free-dom a - way. ___

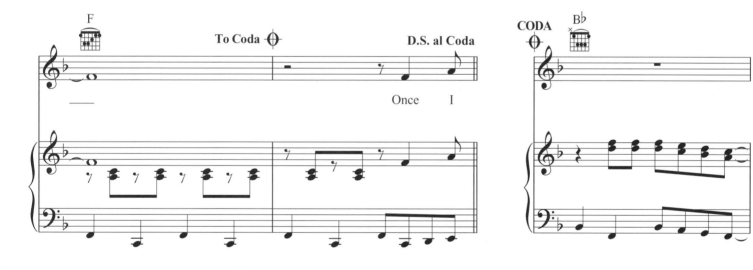

To Coda

D.S. al Coda

Once I

CODA

Yes, no one can take ___ my free-dom a - way. ___

MY MELODY OF LOVE

English and Polish Lyrics by BOBBY VINTON
German Lyrics by GEORGE BUSCHOR
Music by HENRY MAYER

I'm look-ing for a place to go __ so I can be all a-lone __ from thoughts and __ mem-o-
Wish I had a place to hide __ all my sor-row, all my pride. __ I just can't __ get a-

ries, so that when the mu-sic plays I don't go back to the days __
long 'cause the love, once so fine, keeps on hurt-in' all the time. __

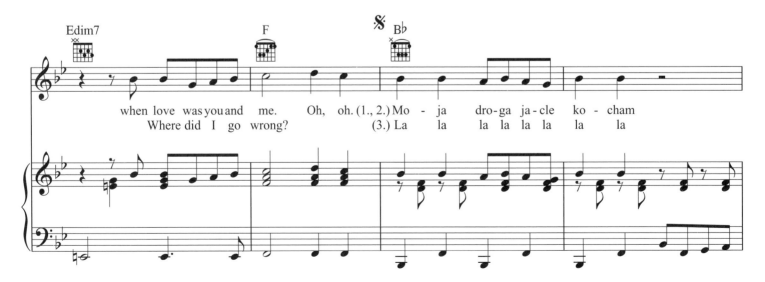

when love was you and me. Oh, oh. (1., 2.) Mo - ja dro-ga ja-cle ko - cham
Where did I go wrong? (3.) La la la la la la la la

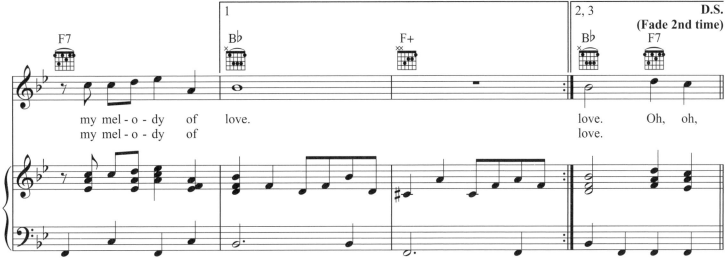

NO BEER TODAY

Words and Music by
HANK HALLER

Bright Polka

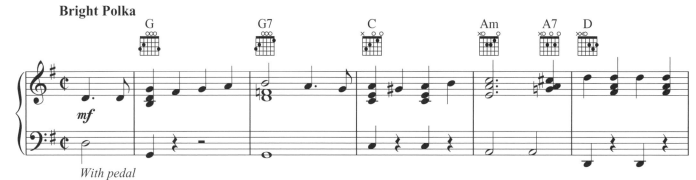

We were driv-ing through a town on a

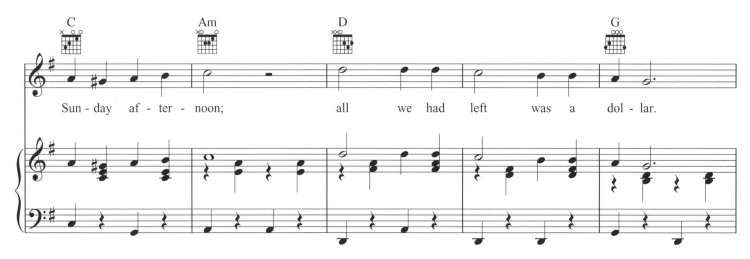

Sun-day af-ter-noon; all we had left was a dol-lar.

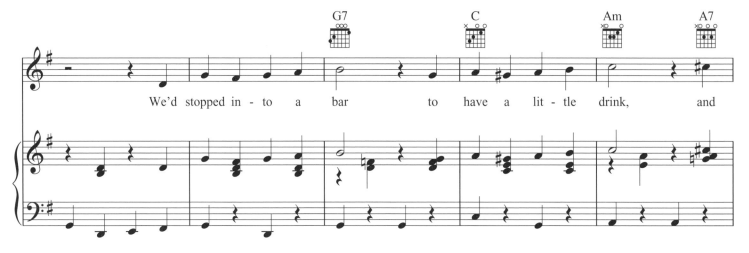

We'd stopped in-to a bar to have a lit-tle drink, and

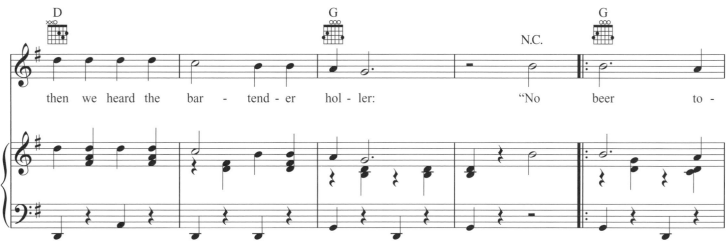

then we heard the bar-tend-er hol-ler: "No beer to-

day! No beer to-day! You can't buy beer on Sun-day.

No beer to-day! No beer to-day! You've

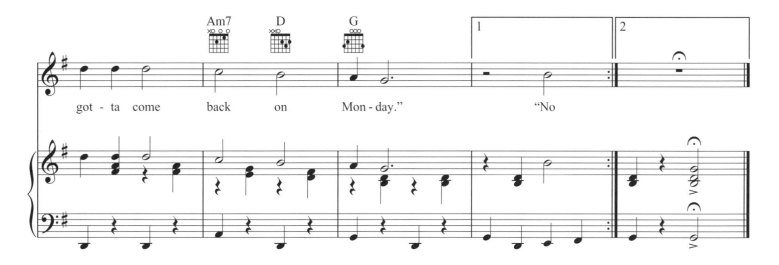

got-ta come back on Mon-day." "No

PENNSYLVANIA POLKA

Words and Music by LESTER LEE
and ZEKE MANNERS

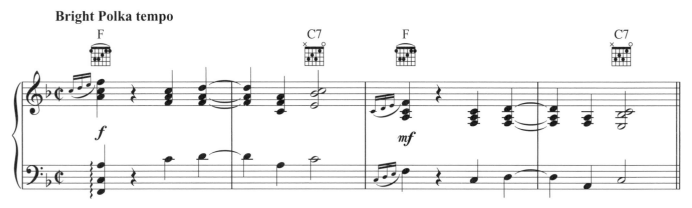

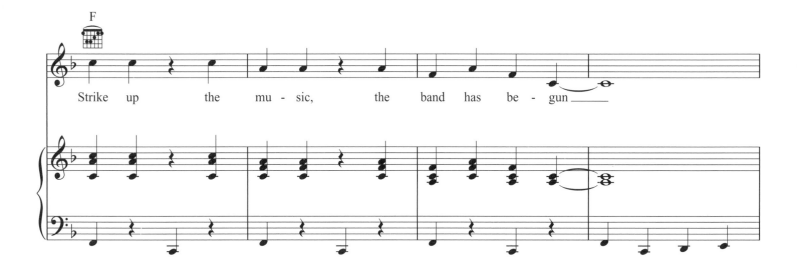

Strike up the mu-sic, the band has be-gun _____

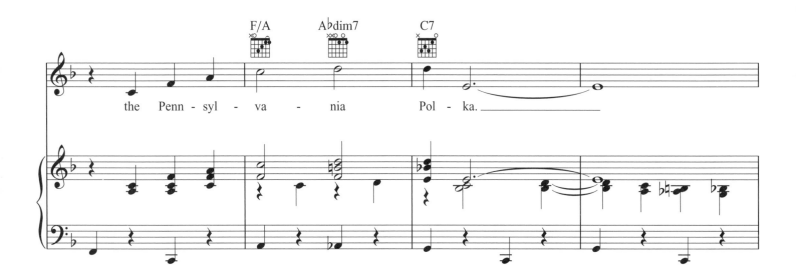

the Penn-syl-va-nia Pol-ka. _____

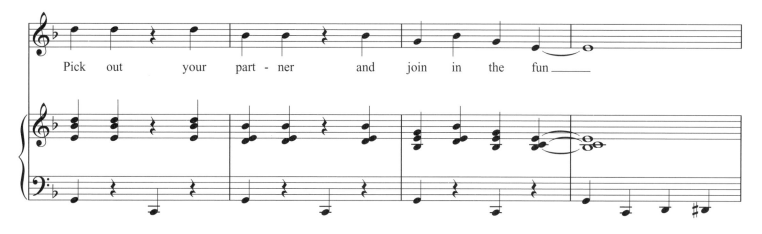

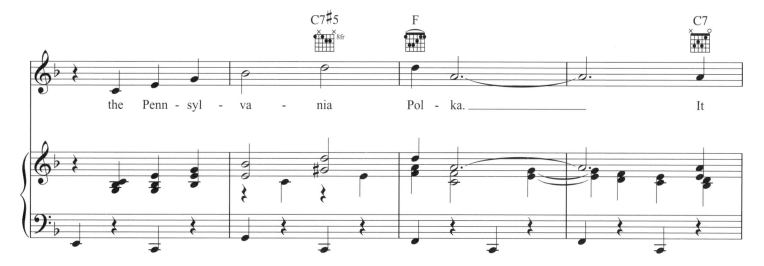

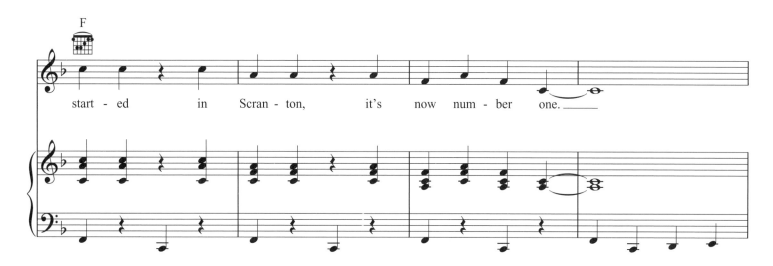

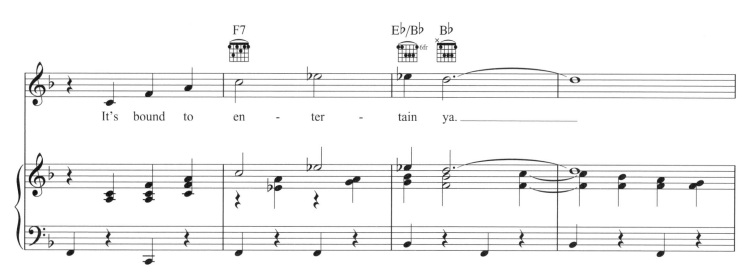

Ev - 'ry - bod - y has a ma - nia _____ to do the

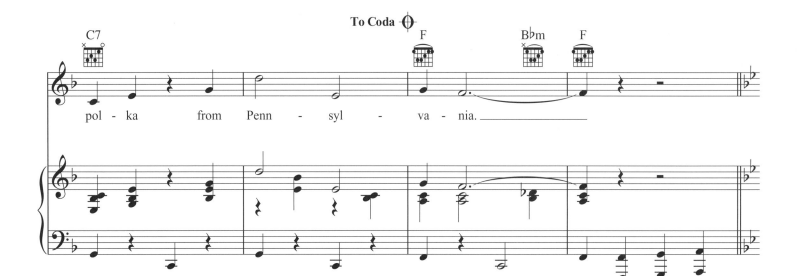

pol - ka from Penn - syl - va - nia. _____

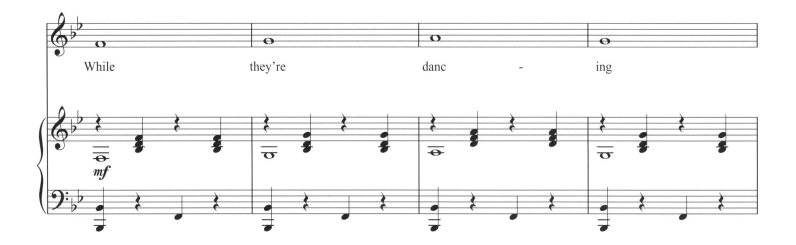

While they're danc - ing

ev - 'ry - bod - y's cares are quick - ly gone.

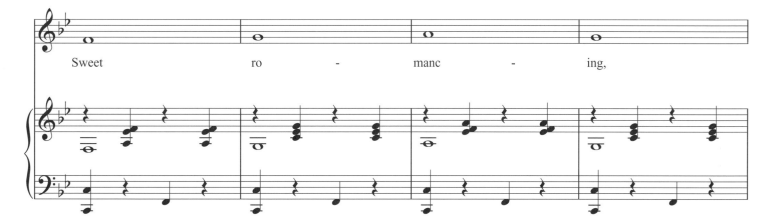

Sweet ro - manc - ing,

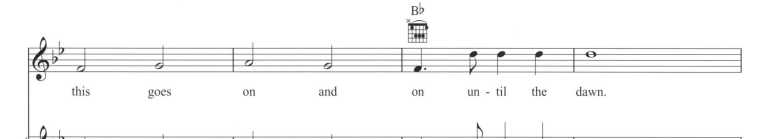

this goes on and on un - til the dawn.

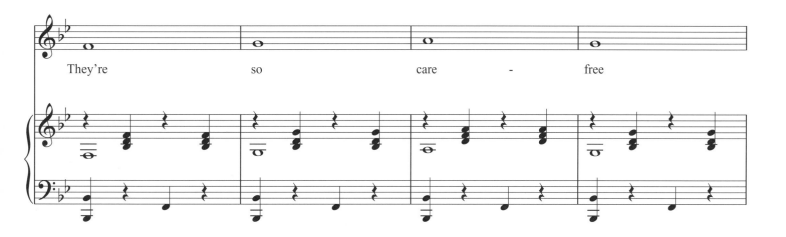

They're so care - free

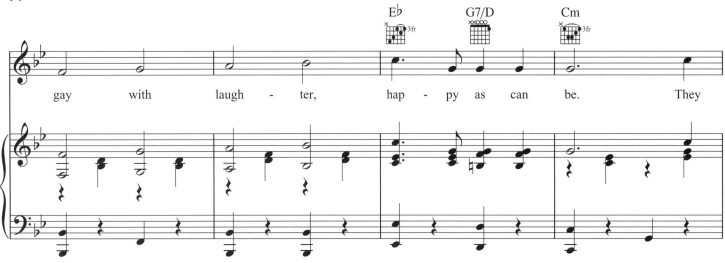

gay with laugh - ter, hap - py as can be. They

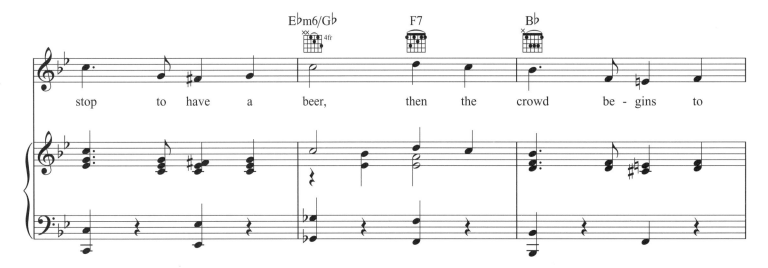

stop to have a beer, then the crowd be - gins to

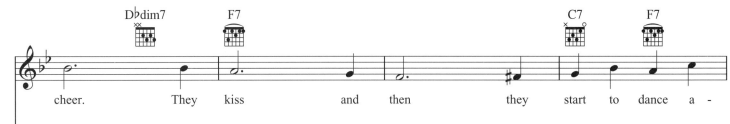

cheer. They kiss and then they start to dance a -

D.C. al Coda

gain:

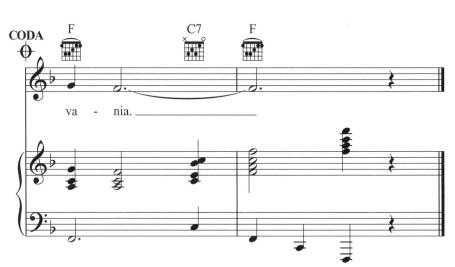

va - nia. _____

PIZZICATO POLKA

By JOHANN STRAUSS, JR.

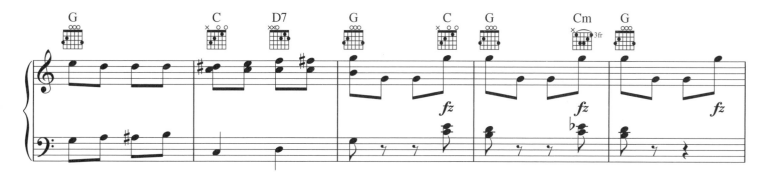

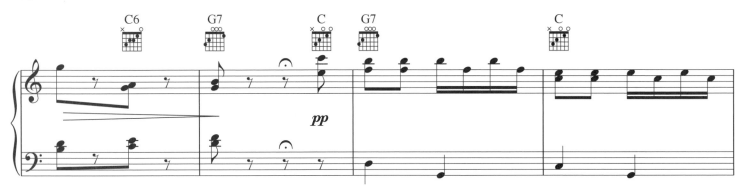

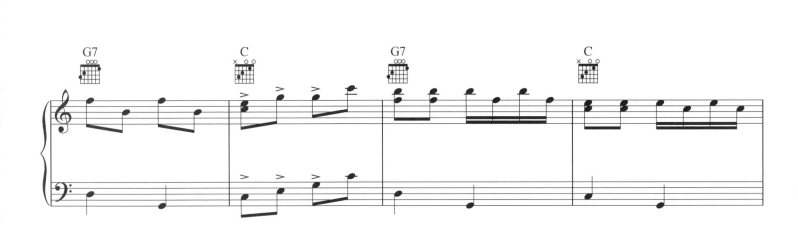

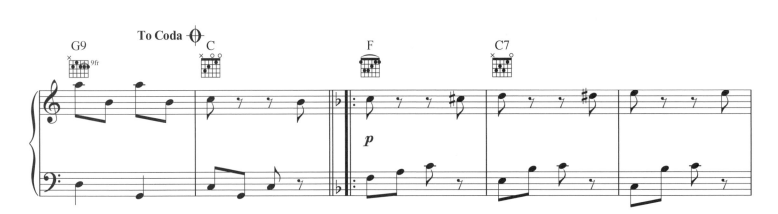

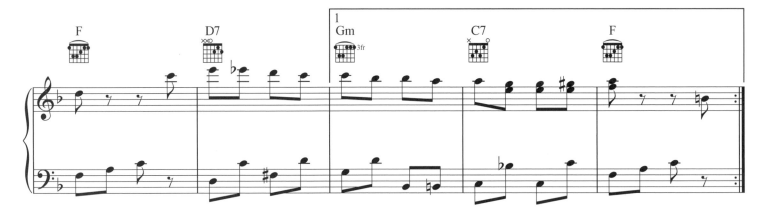

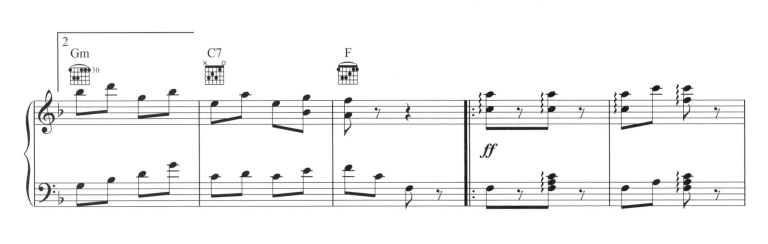

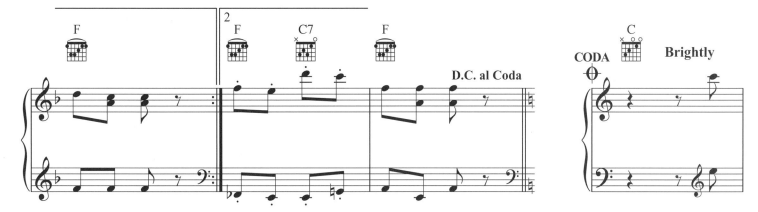

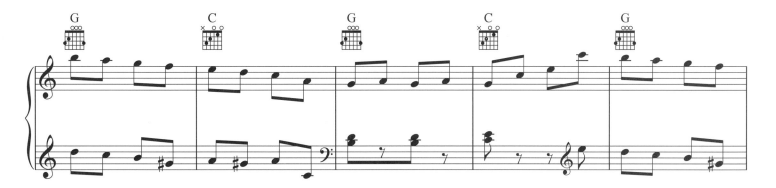

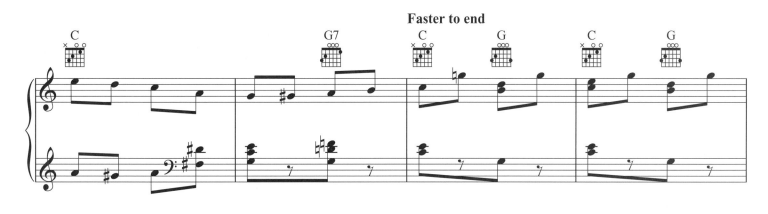

RED WING POLKA

Music by KERRY MILLS
Lyrics by THURLAND CATTAWAY

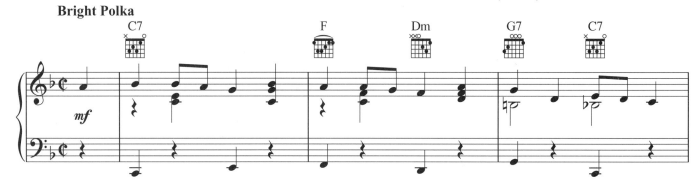

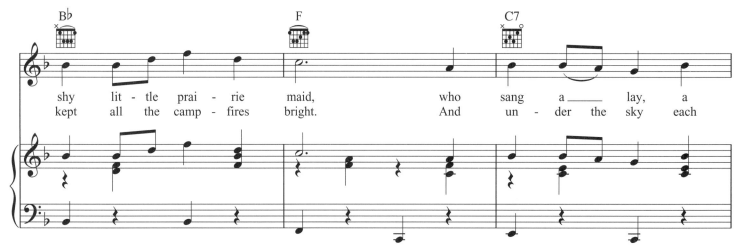

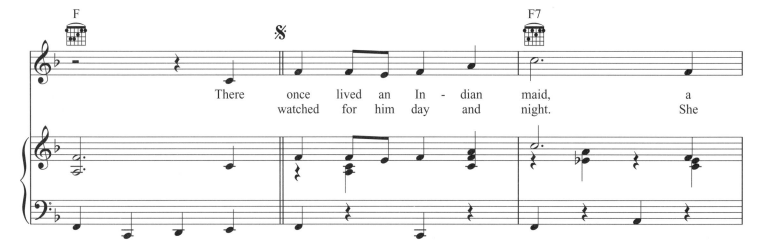

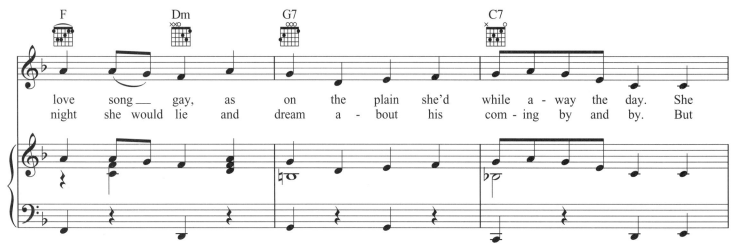

Lyrics (line 2):
There once lived an In-dian maid, a shy lit-tle prai-rie maid, who sang a ___ lay, a love song ___ gay, as on the plain she'd while a-way the day. She

watched for him day and night. She kept all the camp-fires bright. And un-der the sky each night she would lie and dream a-bout his com-ing by and by. But

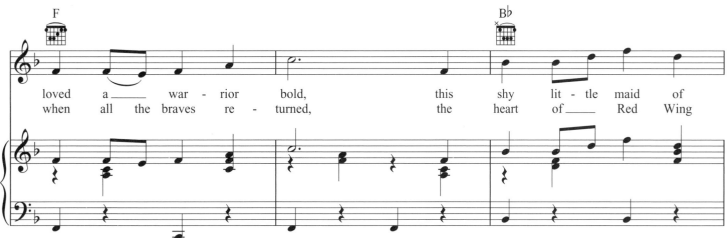

loved a ___ war - rior bold, this shy lit - tle maid of
when all the braves re - turned, the shy heart of ___ Red Wing

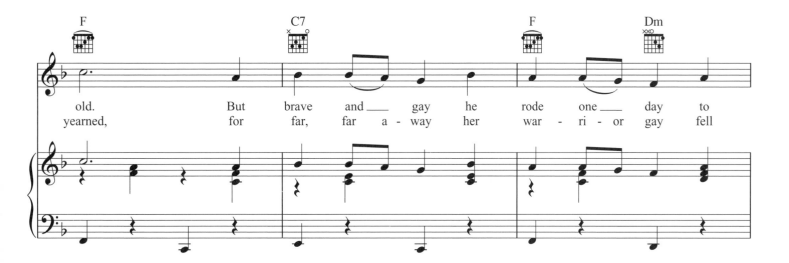

old. But brave and ___ gay he rode one ___ day to
yearned, for far, far a - way her war - ri - or gay fell

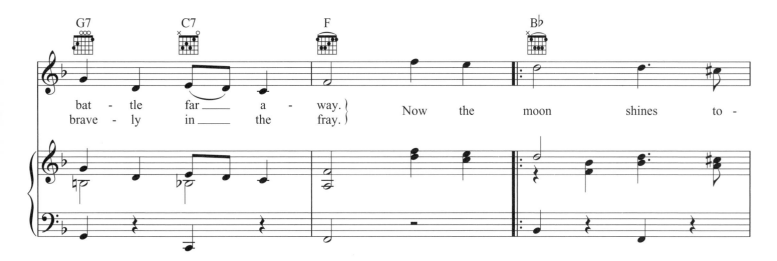

bat - tle far ___ a - way. Now the moon shines to -
brave - ly in ___ the fray.

night on pret - ty Red Wing. ___ The breeze is sigh - ing, ___

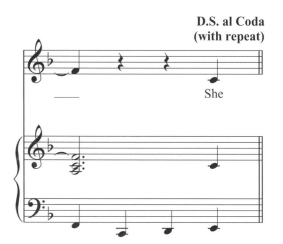

SCHNITZELBANK

German Folksong

82

Kurz und lang un-'er Schnit - zel - bank.

Kurz und lang un-'er Schnit - zel - bank.

Additional Lyrics

2. Ei du schöne, ei du schöne,
   Ei du schöne Schnitzelbank.
   Ist das nicht ein Hin und Her?
   Ja, das ist ein Hin und Her.
   Ist das nicht eine Lichtputzschere?
   Ja, das ist eine Lichtputzschere.
   Lichtputzschere, Hin und Her,
   Kurz und lang un'er Schnitzelbank.

3. Ei du schöne, ei du schöne,
   Ei du schöne Schnitzelbank.
   Ist das nicht ein gold'ner Ring?
   Ja, das ist ein gold'ner Ring.
   Ist das nicht ein schönes Ding?
   Ja, das ist ein schönes Ding.
   Schönes Ding, gold'ner Ring, Lichtputzschere,
   Hin und Her, Kurz und lang un'er Schnitzelbank.

4. Ei du schöne, ei du schöne,
   Ei du schöne Schnitzelbank.
   Ist das nicht ein Krum und Grad?
   Ja, das ist ein Krum und Grad.
   Ist das nicht ein Wagenrad?
   Ja, das ist ein Wagenrad.
   Wagenrad, Krum und Grad,
   Schönes Ding, gold'ner Ring,
   Lichtputzschere, Hin und Her,
   Kurz und lang un'er Schnitzelbank.

5. Ei du schöne, ei du schöne,
   Ei du schöne Schnitzelbank.
   Ist das nicht ein Geisenbock?
   Ja, das ist ein Geisenbock.
   Ist das nicht ein Reifenrock?
   Ja, das ist ein Reifenrock.
   Reifenrock, Geisenbock, Wagenrad,
   Krum und Grad, Schönes Ding,
   Gold'ner Ring, Lichtputzschere, Hin und Her,
   Kurz und lang un'er Schnitzelbank.

6. Ei du schöne, ei du schöne,
   Ei du schöne Schnitzelbank.
   Ist das nicht eine gute Wurst?
   Ja, das ist eine gute Wurst.
   Ist das nicht ein großer Durst?
   Ja, das ist ein großer Durst.
   Großer Durst, gute Wurst,
   Reifenrock, Geisenbock, Wagenrad,
   Krum und Grad, Schönes Ding,
   Gold'ner Ring, Lichtputzschere, Hin und Her,
   Kurz und lang un'er Schnitzelbank.

THERE IS A TAVERN IN THE TOWN

Traditional Drinking Song

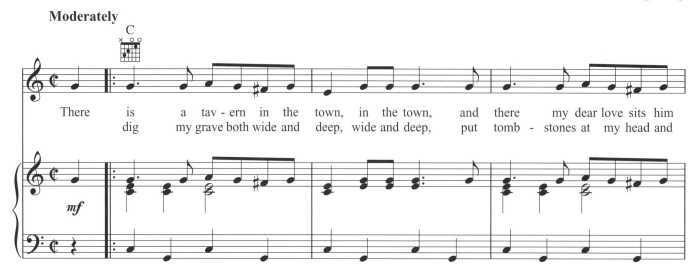

There is a tav-ern in the town, in the town, and there my dear love sits him
dig my grave both wide and deep, wide and deep, put tomb - stones at my head and

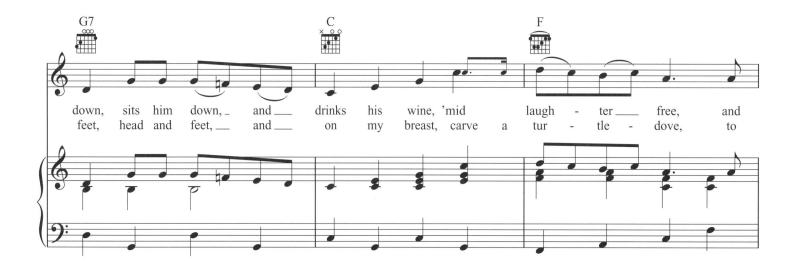

down, sits him down, _ and _ drinks his wine, 'mid laugh - ter _ free, and
feet, head and feet, _ and _ on my breast, carve a tur - tle - dove, to

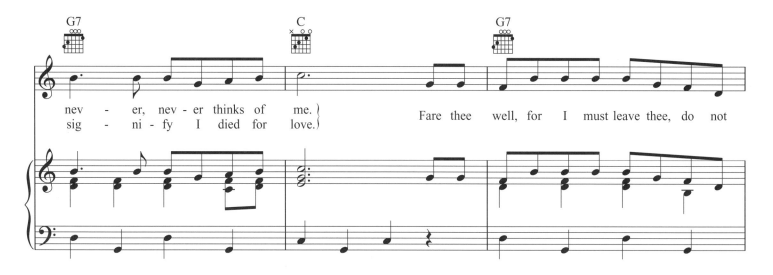

nev - er, nev - er thinks of me. }
sig - ni - fy I died for love. }

Fare thee well, for I must leave thee, do not

let the part - ing grieve thee, and re - mem - ber that the best of friends must part, must part. A -

dieu, a - dieu, kind friends, a - dieu, a - dieu, a - dieu, I can no long - er stay with

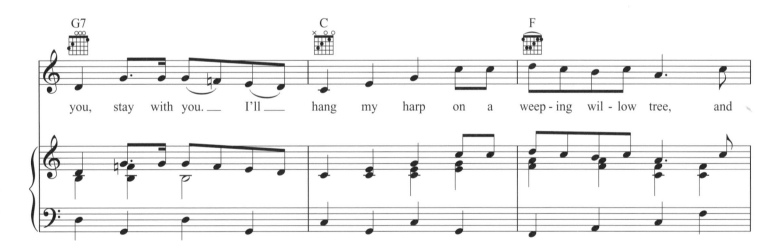

you, stay with you.___ I'll ___ hang my harp on a weep - ing wil - low tree, and

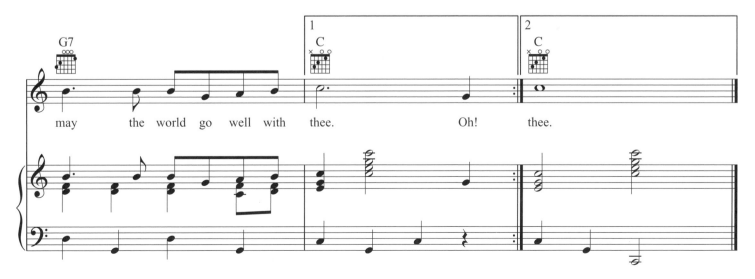

may the world go well with thee. Oh! thee.

TIC-TOCK POLKA

Lyric by S. GUSKI and R.J. MARTINO
Music by G. LAMA

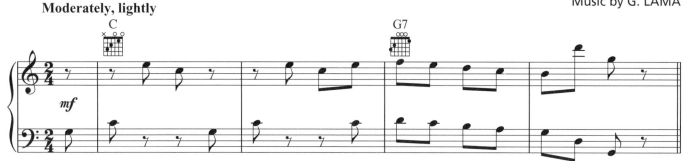

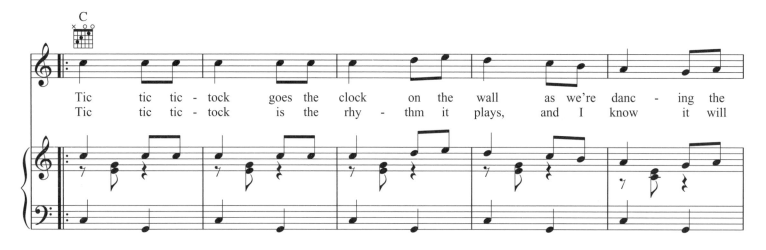

Tic tic tic - tock goes the clock on the wall as we're danc - ing the
Tic tic tic - tock is the rhy - thm it plays, and I know it will

eve - ning a - way. _____ Tic tic tic - tock goes my heart with the
make you feel blue. _____ Tic tic tic - tock goes my heart with the

clock, beat - ing time while the mu - sic is gay. _____
clock. Don't they know I am

TOO FAT POLKA
(She's Too Fat for Me)

Words and Music by ROSS MacLEAN
and ARTHUR RICHARDSON

Bright Polka

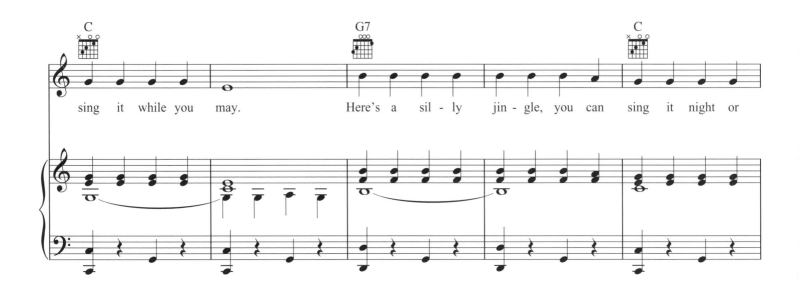

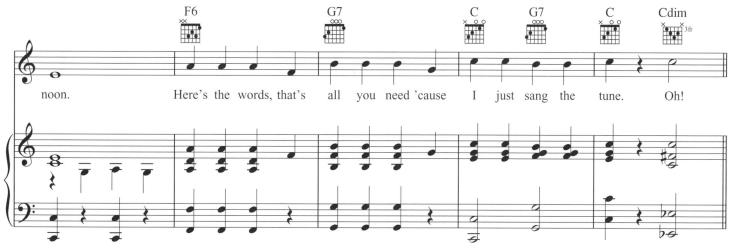

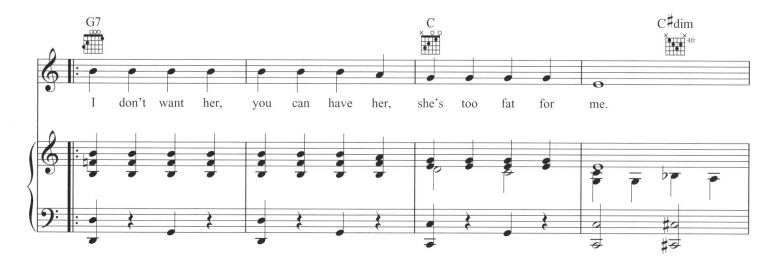

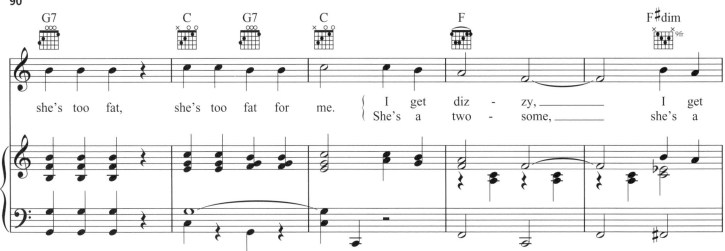

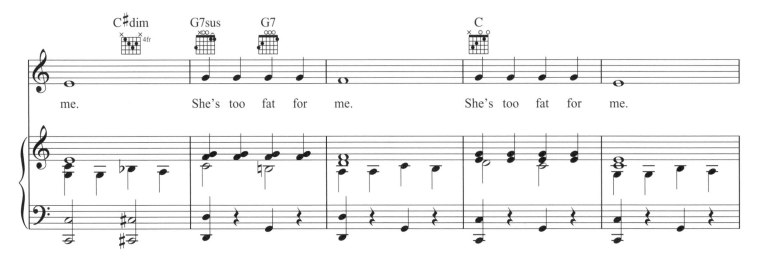

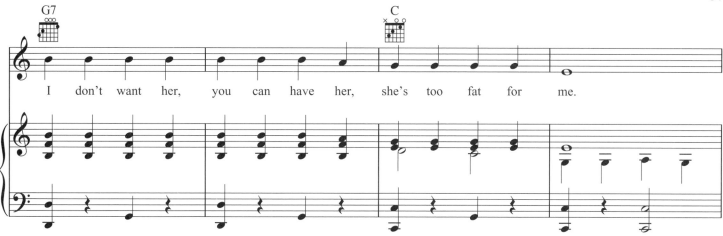

I don't want her, you can have her, she's too fat for me.

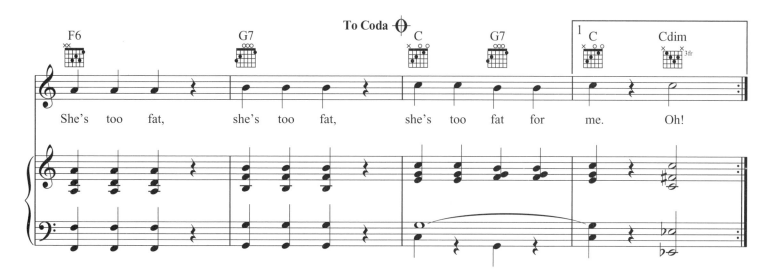

She's too fat, she's too fat, she's too fat for me. Oh!

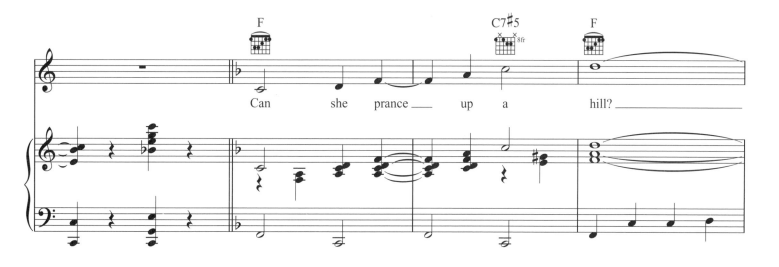

me.

Can she prance _ up a hill? _

92

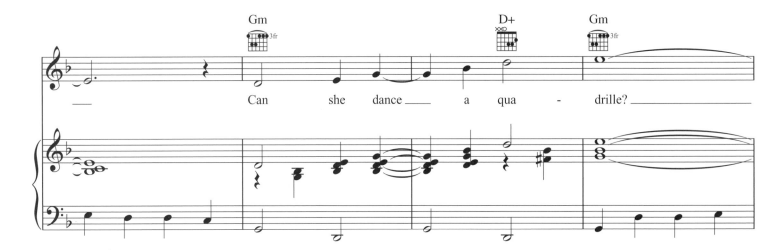

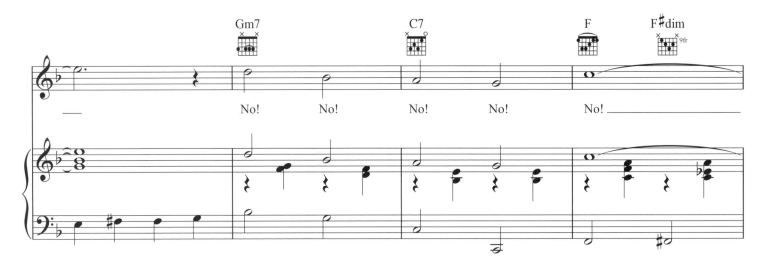

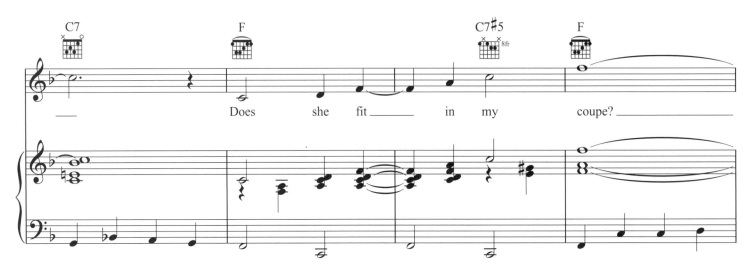

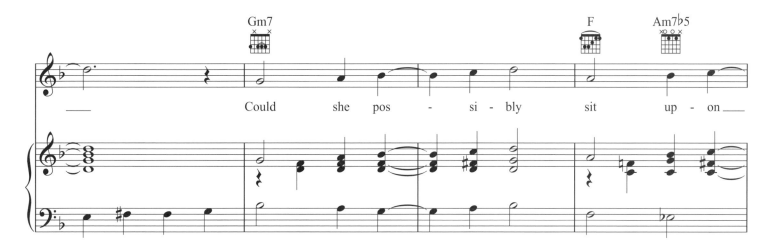

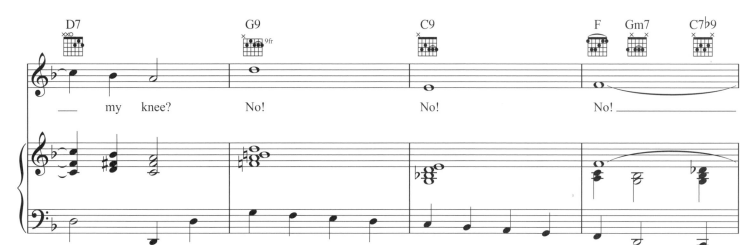

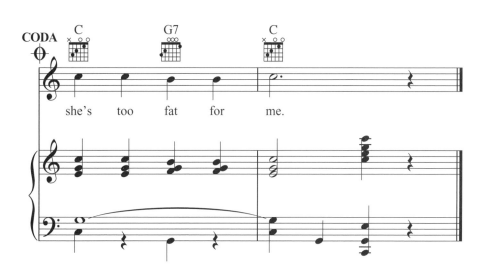

VICT'RY POLKA

Words by SAMMY CAHN
Music by JULE STYNE

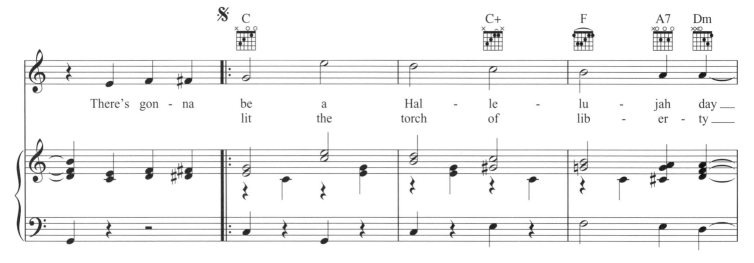

There's gon-na be a Hal - le - lu - jah day
lit the torch of lib - er - ty

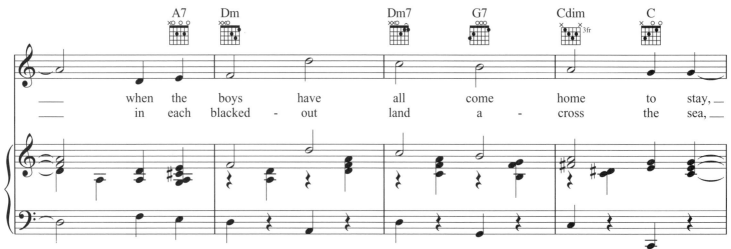

when the boys have all come home to stay,
in each blacked - out land a - cross the sea,

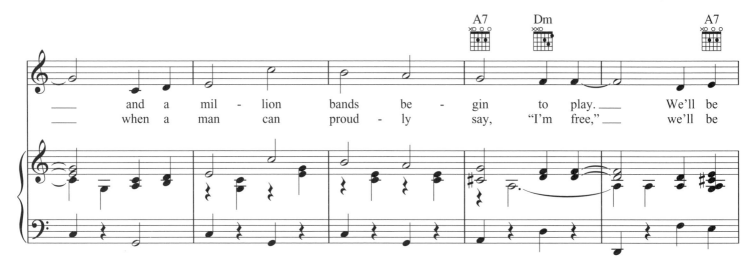

and a mil - lion bands be - gin to play. We'll be
when a man can proud - ly say, "I'm free," we'll be

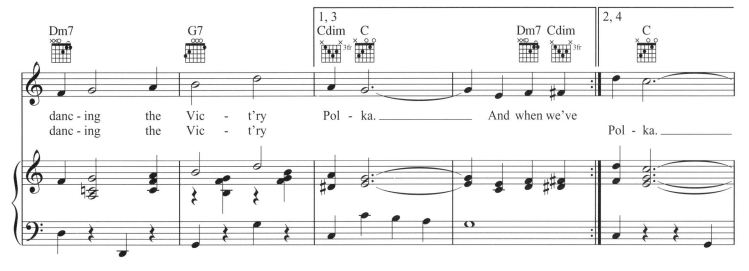

danc - ing the Vic - t'ry Pol - ka. ____ And when we've
danc - ing the Vic - t'ry Pol - ka. ____

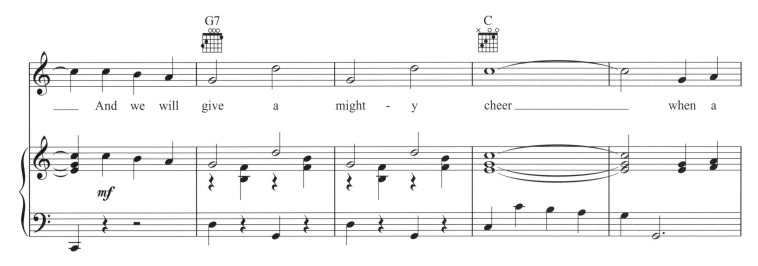

____ And we will give a might - y cheer ____ when a

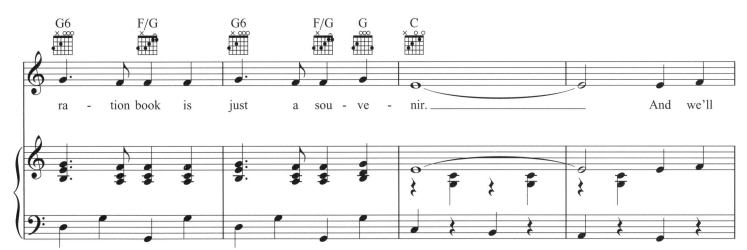

ra - tion book is just a sou - ve - nir. ____ And we'll

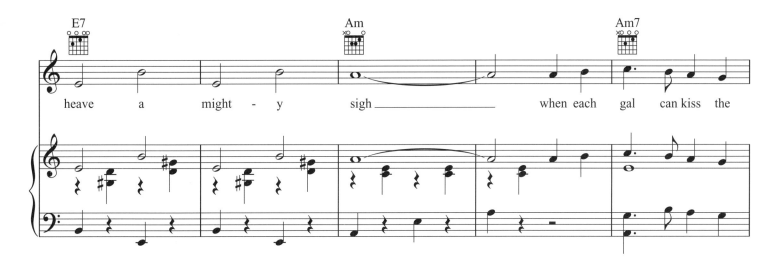

heave a might - y sigh ____ when each gal can kiss the

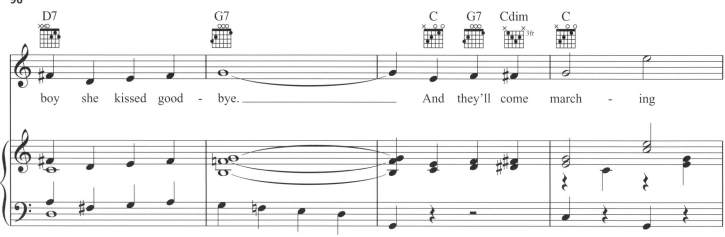

boy she kissed good - bye._____ And they'll come march - ing

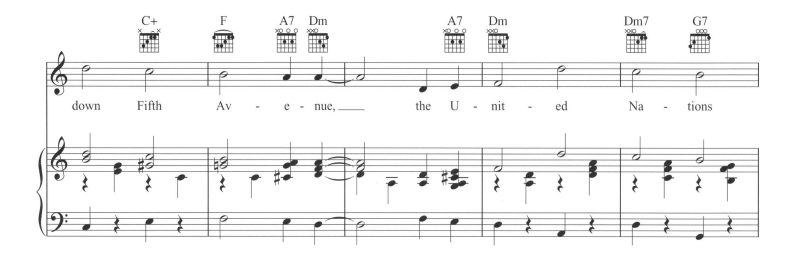

down Fifth Av - e - nue,____ the U - nit - ed Na - tions

in re - view.____ When this love - ly dream has all come true,_

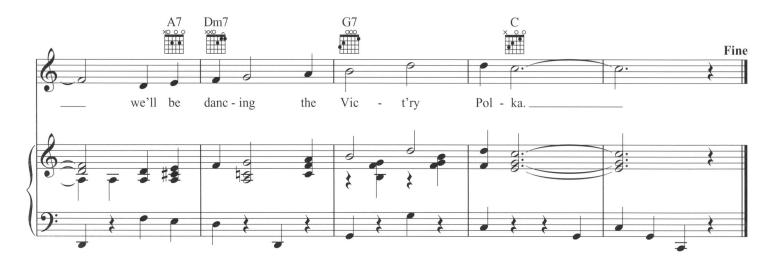

____ we'll be danc - ing the Vic - t'ry Pol - ka._____

Patter (Marciale)

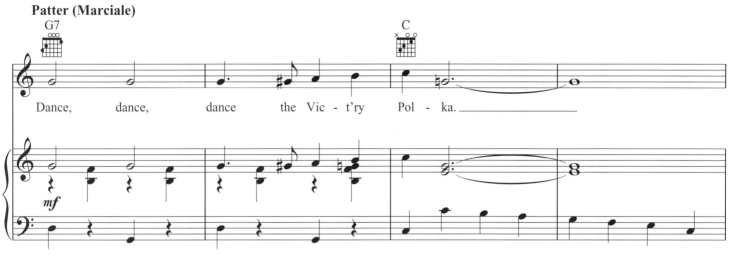

Dance, dance, dance the Vic - t'ry Pol - ka.

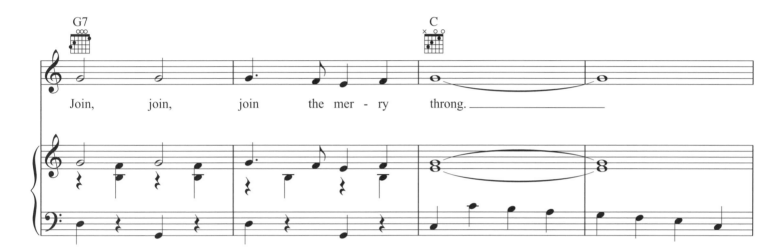

Join, join, join the mer - ry throng.

Sing, sing, sing the Vic - t'ry Pol - ka. _____ Raise your

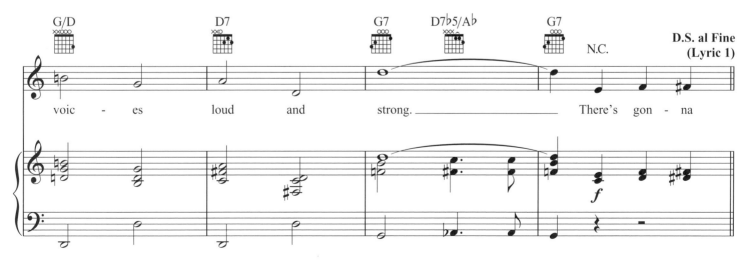

voic - es loud and strong. _____ There's gon - na

D.S. al Fine
(Lyric 1)

TINKER POLKA

Traditional

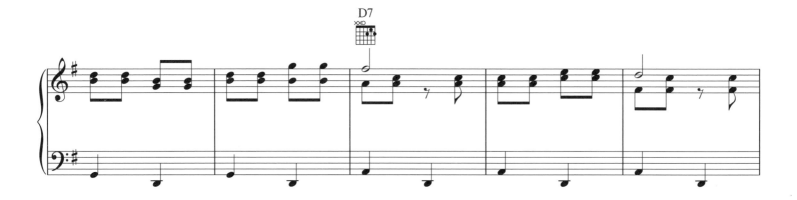

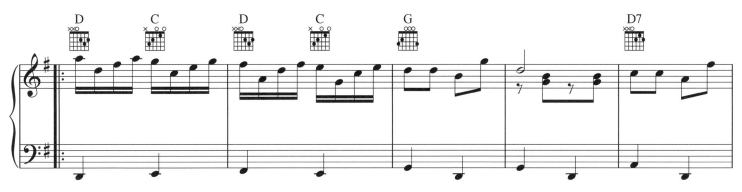

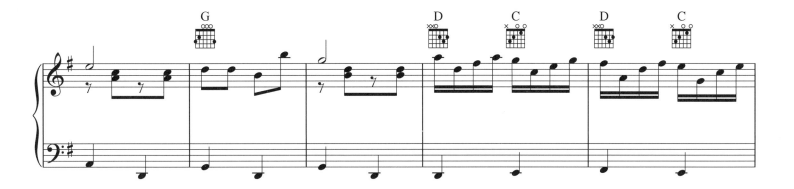

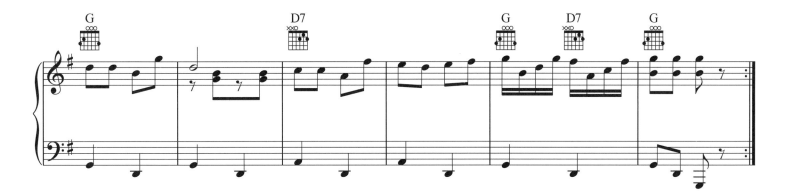

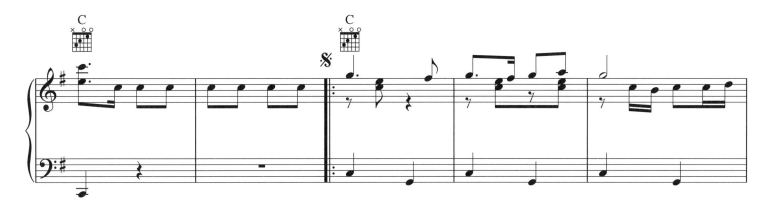

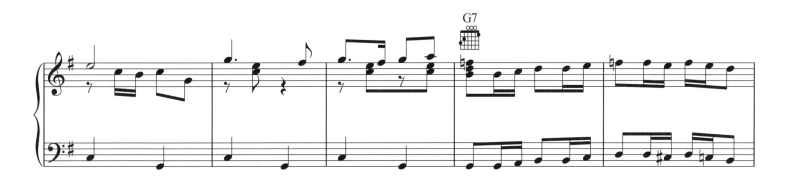

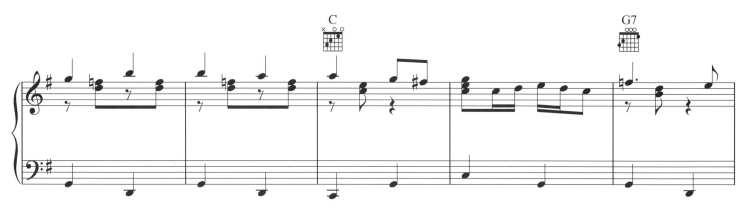

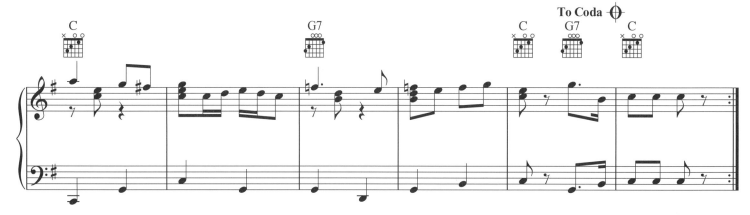

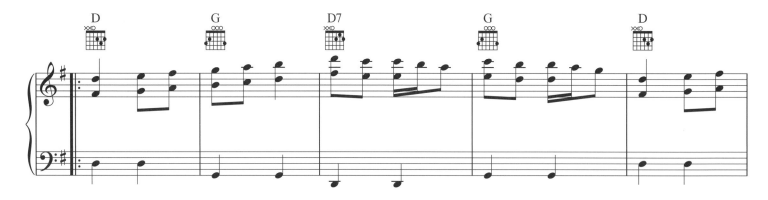

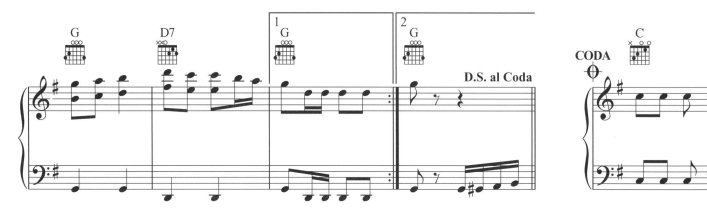

Classic Collections of Your Favorite Songs
arranged for piano, voice, and guitar

Irving Berlin Anthology
A comprehensive collection of 61 timeless songs with a bio, song background notes, and photos. Songs include: Always • Blue Skies • Cheek to Cheek • God Bless America • Marie • Puttin' on the Ritz • Steppin' Out with My Baby • There's No Business Like Show Business • White Christmas • (I Wonder Why?) You're Just in Love • and more.
00312493 .... $29.99

The Best Broadway Songs Ever
Features 85 timeless Broadway favorites arranged for piano and voice with guitar chord frames. Songs include: Bring Him Home • Cabaret • I Could Have Danced All Night • Memory • My Favorite Things • On the Street Where You Live • One • People Will Say We're in Love • Popular • Seasons of Love • Send in the Clowns • Somewhere • Sunrise, Sunset • Tomorrow • Try to Remember • Waving Through a Window • What I Did for Love • You'll Be Back • You'll Never Walk Alone • and more.
00291992 .... $29.99

The Best Songs Ever – 9th Edition
Includes 71 all-time hits, including: Always • Bohemian Rhapsody • Candle in the Wind • Defying Gravity • Every Breath You Take • Fly Me to the Moon (In Other Words) • The Girl from Ipanema (Garota De Ipanema) • Hallelujah • Happy • I Dreamed a Dream • Just the Way You Are • Love Me Tender • Memory • My Favorite Things • Night and Day • Over the Rainbow • Piano Man • Satin Doll • Summertime • Tears in Heaven • Unforgettable • What a Wonderful World • Yesterday • You Raise Me Up • and more.
00265721 .... $27.99

The Big Book of Standards
86 classics essential to any music library, including: April in Paris • Autumn in New York • Blue Skies • Cheek to Cheek • Heart and Soul • I Left My Heart in San Francisco • In the Mood • Isn't It Romantic? • Mona Lisa • Moon River • The Nearness of You • Out of Nowhere • Spanish Eyes • Star Dust • Stella by Starlight • That Old Black Magic • They Say It's Wonderful • What Now My Love • and more.
00311667 .... $19.95

The Great American Songbook – The Composers
From Berlin to Gershwin to Rodgers to Waller, this folio features a comprehensive collection of standards from the greatest American composers, along with photos and bios of these masters of song. Includes beloved standards from: Harold Arlen (It's Only a Paper Moon) • Irving Berlin (Blue Skies) • Sammy Cahn (All the Way) • Duke Ellington (Don't Get Around Much Anymore, Mood Indigo) • Dorothy Fields (A Fine Romance) • George Gershwin (Somebody Loves Me) • Johnny Green (Body and Soul) • Jerome Kern (All the Things You Are) • Frank Loesser (Two Sleepy People) • Johnny Mercer (Moon River) • Cole Porter (I've Got You Under My Skin) • Rodgers and Hammerstein (The Surrey with the Fringe on Top) • Rodgers and Hart (My Funny Valentine) • Billy Strayhorn (Satin Doll) • Fats Waller (Ain't Misbehavin') • and many, many more!
00311365 .... $29.99

The Great American Songbook – The Singers
Crooners, wailers, shouters, balladeers: some of our greatest pop vocalists have poured their hearts and souls into the musical gems of the Great American Songbook. This folio features 100 of these classics by Louis Armstrong, Tony Bennett, Rosemary Clooney, Nat "King" Cole, Bing Crosby, Doris Day, Ella Fitzgerald, Judy Garland, Dean Martin, Frank Sinatra, Barbra Streisand, Mel Tormé, and others.
00311433 .... $34.99

I'll Be Seeing You! – 2nd Edition
A salute to the music and memories of WWII, including a year-by-year chronology of events on the homefront, dozens of photos, and 50 radio favorites of the GIs and their families back home, including: Boogie Woogie Bugle Boy • Don't Sit Under the Apple Tree (With Anyone Else But Me) • I Don't Want to Walk Without You • I'll Be Seeing You • Moonlight in Vermont • There's a Star-Spangled Banner Waving Somewhere • You'd Be So Nice to Come Home To • and more.
00311698 .... $22.99

Lounge Music – 2nd Edition
Features over 50 top requests of the martini crowd: All the Way • Fever • I Write the Songs • Misty • Moon River • That's Amore (That's Love) • Yesterday • more.
00310193 .... $15.95

The Henry Mancini Collection
This superb collection includes 45 songs spanning Mancini's illustrious career: Baby Elephant Walk • Breakfast at Tiffany's • Charade • Days of Wine and Roses • Mr. Lucky • Moon River • Peter Gunn • The Pink Panther • A Shot in the Dark • The Thorn Birds • and more.
00313522 .... $19.99

Ladies of Song
This terrific collection includes over 70 songs associated with some of the greatest female vocalists ever recorded. Songs include: Cabaret • Downtown • The First Time Ever I Saw Your Face • God Bless' the Child • If I Were a Bell • My Funny Valentine • One for My Baby (And One More for the Road) • The Way We Were • and many more.
00311948 .... $19.99

The Best of Rodgers & Hammerstein
A capsule of 26 classics from this legendary duo. Songs include: Climb Ev'ry Mountain • Edelweiss • Getting to Know You • I'm Gonna Wash That Man Right Outta My Hair • My Favorite Things • Oklahoma • The Surrey with the Fringe on Top • You'll Never Walk Alone • and more.
00308210 .... $19.99

Torch Songs – 2nd Edition
Sing your heart out with this collection of 59 sultry jazz and big band melancholy masterpieces, including: Angel Eyes • Cry Me a River • I Can't Get Started • I Got It Bad and That Ain't Good • I'm Glad There Is You • Lover Man (Oh, Where Can You Be?) • Misty • My Funny Valentine • Stormy Weather • and many more! 224 pages.
00490446 .... $22.99

Prices, contents, and availability subject to change without notice.
Some products may be unavailable outside the U.S.A.

HAL•LEONARD®
7777 W. BLUEMOUND RD. P.O. BOX 13819 MILWAUKEE, WI 53213

www.halleonard.com